Teaching and Its Predicaments

TEACHING AND ITS PREDICAMENTS

David K. Cohen

HARVARD UNIVERSITY PRESS

Cambridge, Massachusetts, and London, England

2011

Library of Congress Cataloging-in-Publication Data

Cohen, David K., 1934–
Teaching and its predicaments / David K. Cohen.
p. cm.
Includes bibliographical references and index.
ISBN 978-0-674-05110-2 (alk. paper)
1. Teaching.   I. Title.
LB1025.3.C635 2011
371.102—dc22   2011010434

To the memory of my parents,
Eleanor Kastner Cohen and Isadore H. Cohen,
from whom I learned a great deal about predicaments

Contents

Acknowledgments

I began to think about some of the issues in this project in the late 1960s, when my studies of education policy led me to wonder how policy makers viewed teaching, and how well they understood it. That curiosity turned into a serious inquiry about a decade later, when I began to observe teachers at work and read others' accounts of this occupation. This led to more observation, more questions, and studies of teaching and its relation to policy. The analysis in the text that follows developed during several decades, and has been a source of ideas for much of my other work; that slowed this book down but helped to speed other projects along.

The long life of this project also meant that I probably imposed more than ordinarily on friends, family, and colleagues. They were unfailingly generous. Very particular thanks are due to Magdalene Lampert, for our wonderful life together has included, among many other things, a long-running discussion of teaching, the results of which pervade this book. This is in many respects a joint project. Special thanks also are due to Deborah Loewenberg Ball, for our work together has been a pleasure, and an important source of many ideas in the chapters that follow. After so many years and so much conversation and work, I can no

longer clearly distinguish where their ideas leave off and mine begin. I also owe sincere thanks to close colleagues, students, and members of my family, for their encouragement and helpful comments on various versions of this manuscript at various times: Tony Bryk, Daniel Chazan, Lisa Cohen, Helen Featherstone, Jay Featherstone, Francesca Forzani, Simona Goldin, Pam Grossman, Patricio Herbst, Heather C. Hill, Marvin Hoffman, Mary Kennedy, Charles E. Lindblom, Milbrey Wallin McLaughlin, Mary H. Metz, Mary Catherine O'Connor, Donald Peurach, Seneca Rosenberg, Lee Shulman, Jim Stigler, Gary Sykes, Janet A. Weiss, Suzanne Wilson, and Alida Zweidler-McKay. The interest and encouragement of Elizabeth Knoll, Senior Editor for the Behavioral Sciences and Law at Harvard University Press, helped to find this book a fine publisher, and a few of her pointed inquiries convinced me to stop revising and send the manuscript on its way. The sharp-eyed copyediting of Charles N. Eberline and production editing of Melody Negron of Westchester Book Services saved that manuscript from many mistakes.

Several educational organizations supported this work. The College of Education at Michigan State University, and the School of Education and the Ford School of Public Policy at the University of Michigan provided faculty appointments that made it possible for me to sustain work on this project. The Mandel Foundation in Jerusalem has for many years provided me with time to work in an organization centrally concerned with teaching, and opportunities to try out some of my ideas on colleagues there. I am especially grateful to the late Seymour Fox and to Annette Hochstein—past presidents of the Mandel Foundation in Jerusalem—for these opportunities, and to Mort Mandel for his generous support of the foundation that helped to sustain my work.

Chapter 5 draws on an essay that was published in the *Oxford Review of Education* (Fall 2008), under the title "Knowledge and Teaching." Chapters 1 and 2 draw on material that was published under the title "Professions of Human Improvement: Predicaments of Teaching," in *Educational Deliberations: Studies in Education Dedicated to Shlomo (Seymour) Fox* (Jerusalem: Keter, 2008).

TEACHING AND ITS PREDICAMENTS

I

IMPROVE TEACHING?

The developed world has seen a remarkable escalation of ambition for schools. Policy makers and some educators in the 1980s began to say that schools must offer intellectually challenging instruction that is deeply rooted in the academic disciplines. Under Margaret Thatcher, John Major, and Tony Blair, British schooling was revamped to exert much greater pressure on academic work. Reformers and policy makers in the United States also urged more thoughtful and intellectually ambitious instruction and argued that students must become independent thinkers and enterprising problem solvers.

Ambitious changes in politics and policy were made to achieve these goals. The British government centralized influence over state-maintained schools and placed much more stress on examinations and common curricula. A few states in the United States instituted aggressive systems of testing and accountability on the grounds that state tests would push instruction to greater heights, and many more followed suit after the passage of President Clinton's education reforms in the mid-1990s. Prominent politicians, businessmen, and analysts argued that schools should be judged by their results in student performance, not by the money that they had. These

ideas got an additional brisk boost from the passage of No Child Left Behind early in George W. Bush's presidency.

These policies and ideas seemed hopeful to some and unwise to others, but whatever one's view, they marked serious change. Resource allocation had been the chief method to judge schools' quality in the United States, teachers had had considerable leeway, and there was no formal accountability for students' learning. One problem that caught my attention, common across efforts to reform many different systems, was political. Power and authority have been dispersed by the growth of powerful interest groups—such as teachers' unions in Britain, Israel, and Japan or state and local authorities in the United States—or by federalism, as in Australia, or by a combination of these things in the United States. Could state or national agencies mobilize the influence to steer teaching and learning in thousands of classrooms when authority was so fractured?

A second problem was educational and arose from the idea that teaching and learning should be much more thoughtful and demanding. Teachers are urged to help students understand mathematical concepts, interpret serious literature, write creatively about their ideas and experiences, and converse thoughtfully about history and social studies. Whatever we think of these ambitions in principle, they were unfamiliar in practice in most U.S. schools. Most teaching was frontal, centered on teachers, and aside from some crack academic classes, intellectual demands were modest. Few elementary-school teachers had deep knowledge of any academic subject, and the ambitious instruction that reformers proposed had been confined mostly to protected enclaves in a few public and private secondary schools. Could any authority move teaching and learning far from such established practice?

Perhaps. But if intellectual excitement was to be the meat and potatoes of teaching, much would have to change. What might it

take to transform teaching from a largely routine and unimaginative practice into an intellectually ambitious and adventurous enterprise? Such changes had been tried with little success earlier in U.S. history. Why had they been so difficult?

By World War II teaching already was America's most investigated profession, the object of many studies, much criticism, and repeated proposals for reform. The postwar explosion of higher education, the consequent growth of the social sciences, and increasing efforts at school reform fueled a huge growth in research on education, and more investigations and reform proposals followed. Investigators scrutinized teachers' education, the conditions of their work, the unions they joined, the salaries they earned, how and why they made decisions, and many related subjects. As I worked on this project, I read many of these studies, but I gradually saw that even in this accelerating blizzard of research there was little about the work of teaching itself. Researchers probed the occupation from dozens of angles and produced boxcar loads of studies, but only a few asked the rudimentary questions: What sort of an endeavor is teaching? What kinds of problems must teachers solve, and how do they solve them? And what would it take to solve them in ways that promote ambitious teaching and learning?

Those three questions summarize the assignment that I set for myself. My answers are presented in the chapters that follow. They will not help readers learn how to teach, nor will they inform them about "findings." They will, I hope, help them understand teaching and its sister occupations. My analysis has been informed by my observation of elementary- and high-school classes, by interviews with teachers, by reading many other accounts of teaching and related work, and by conversations with colleagues who study teaching, but most of all by sustained thought.

3

2

HUMAN IMPROVEMENT

Teaching seems plain enough. An older or more educated person holds forth to those younger or less knowledgeable. Children sit at small desks, adolescents slouch in lecture halls, and grown-ups gather in semicircles. The older or more learned person almost always stands in front and almost always talks. So when I ask, "What sort of endeavor is teaching?" the answer seems simple: one in which knowledge and skills are transmitted.

All true, but not all that is true. One might also say that teachers try to improve their students' minds, souls, and habits. There are many important differences among such improvers. Some teach in kindergarten, while others do so in graduate school. Some teach subatomic physics, others inculcate religious beliefs, and, in religious schools, teachers may do both. If the range of teachers' aims is amazing, so are the situations in which they labor. Some work in one-room schools, while others instruct in universities that enroll forty thousand students. Some tutor a single student, while others face four thousand. But throughout all these differences, teachers work at a profession of human improvement. Like psychotherapists, social workers, pastors, and organization developers, they work directly on other humans in efforts to better their minds, lives, work, and organizations.

4

Human improvement occupations share extraordinary ambitions. Workers seek to improve skills, deepen insights, broaden understanding, cope with feelings, take another's point of view, and increase honesty. These are occupations in which workers attempt to transform minds, enrich human capabilities, and change behavior. Learning is central to all of them, and in all it is seen as the key to betterment. Workers regularly remind us that their work is crucial to modern life. Teachers cultivate practical intelligence, theoretical reason, and the capacity to solve problems, without which many argue that a modern economy would falter or collapse. Organizational consultants improve effectiveness, productivity, and even honesty in organizations. Some of these occupations, like psychotherapy and organization development, are quite new, the progeny of the idea of progress that has flourished in Europe and North America since the Enlightenment. Others, like teaching and pastoral work, are ancient but have been reconceived in light of modern ambitions.

Workers in all these unusual trades face several common predicaments. One can best be put as a paradox: although special expertise is practitioners' chief qualification to work with clients, expertise is never enough. No matter how well educated and professionally informed they may be, workers frequently have no conclusive expert solutions, even to many basic problems. Schoolteachers and academic experts regularly disagree about the purposes of practice. Many argue that teachers should instill obedience and respect for authority in students, but others insist that they should cultivate critical intelligence and the disposition to question authority. Some contend that students should learn the basics, while others argue for much more intellectually elevated work. There is no scientifically conclusive way to decide such disputes; indeed, these disputes thrive in social science, as well as in popular discourse.

Americans also dispute the best ways to reach these academic goals. Some argue that hands-on experience and practical work are the best road to knowledge, while others urge rigorous academic study. Deep disagreements exist even among advocates of rigorous study. Some argue for sustained work on academic content, while others insist on the importance of learning processes, critical thinking, or reading strategies.[1] Observers and evaluators also disagree about how to judge success. In teaching reading or arithmetic, as in any profession of human improvement, what strikes some as the same improvement—for example, learning two-digit multiplication—can be defined in different ways, each plausible from some perspective. We can identify different means to achieve any improvement, each supported by some observers and practitioners, and each backed by more or less evidence of success. Professional knowledge and social science inform these views, but conclusive evidence is rare.[2] Practitioners in every human improvement profession struggle with similar problems, as do commentators on these professions; expertise is essential to good practice, but it also is essentially inadequate.[3]

Some readers may demur and say that the progress of science or professional education will solve the problem. Prediction about matters of this sort is impossible, but the historical record is not encouraging. Uncertainty and dispute about human improvement have not diminished in the century just past, during which the entire enterprise expanded enormously, professional education in human improvement occupations grew into a vast undertaking, and social research was applied on an increasing scale. Contrary to the hopes of many advocates for the saving power of science, these developments were accompanied by increasing dispute and uncertainty. As each profession prospered, so did rival schools of thought and practice within it. Jung and Freud invented the first great sys-

tems of psychoanalysis. Although psychotherapy grew, much of the expansion was in contending treatments, and much of the professional literature was marked by disputes about them. As early skepticism about the efficacy of psychic therapy declined, it was replaced by critiques of particular treatments and later by bitter attacks on the entire therapeutic enterprise. One particularly striking example is the view, advanced by leading psychiatrists, that madness is essentially rational and that psychotherapy is a cause of human misery rather than its cure.[4]

A similar story can be told about teaching. Disputes about the best ways to instruct are as old as public education. In the United States, some educators and divines in the 1700s saw instruction as a fierce struggle with depravity, while others saw it as a gentle cultivation of humanity's goodness. The birth of public schools in Boston in the 1830s and 1840s was accompanied by a fierce battle between reformers and schoolmen about whether instruction should be grounded in the rigorous recitation of facts in books or in efforts to solve "real" practical problems. These old divisions are still with us, but a myriad of other theories and practices have sprung up in the intervening decades, including, among others, Montessori education, anarchist schools, progressivism, behavior modification, open education, free schools, and Christian fundamentalist schools. Levels of education, literacy, and humanity in instruction have grown greatly since Horace Mann campaigned for public schools in the 1840s, but so have competing ideas about instruction and attacks on teaching as a cause of oppression and ignorance. The progress of education has been accompanied by increasingly bitter critiques and multiplying disputes about whether education has improved or weakened. Some commentators portray schooling as a vicious attack on innocent children or a calculated

means of holding entire populations in intellectual and political bondage, ideas that were almost entirely absent from early debates about public education.[5] The growth of formal education evidences expanding faith in the possibilities of human improvement and increasing doubt about teachers' capacity to deliver the goods.

That paradox has been vividly displayed in recent efforts at school reform. Since the mid-1980s state and federal governments have pressed schools, especially those that serve disadvantaged students, to improve. Policy makers insist that schools should eliminate gaps in average achievement between advantaged and disadvantaged students and between African American or Hispanic and white students. That goal is unprecedentedly ambitious, not only because the policies propose to judge schools by results rather than by the quality of instruction but also because inequality in students' social and economic backgrounds and in their schools' educational resources is great. But the same policies that express extraordinary faith in the schools' capability for human improvement argue that public schools have seriously failed. If they have failed as badly as the policies assert, though, how can they be expected to produce dramatically different results? The answers—charter schools and school "turnaround" chief among them—combine the view that many public schools are hopelessly incapable, with the idea that effective education can be achieved by changing organization and leadership. The evidence that nearly half of charter schools do less to boost students' performance than comparable local public schools does not bear out the optimism, but it has done little to blunt advocates' pessimism about public schools and their optimism about charter schools.

The paradox of expertise is evident also in the proliferation of self-help improvement schemes. Books, magazines, tapes, and video

recordings promise emotional peace without therapists: we need only perform therapy on ourselves. Various experts propose education without teachers: we need only read manuals or use computers. Managers are urged to improve their organizations in five minutes by reading a book or listening to a tape. These schemes testify to both an irrepressible faith in human improvement and deep doubts about practitioners' expertise. If we can find peace without therapists, education without teachers, and decent organizations without consultants, how important are practitioners, and how weighty is their expertise?

To date, the progress of human improvement and expanded knowledge about it seem to have increased uncertainty rather than diminishing it and to have complicated practitioners' work rather than simplifying it. Practitioners must solve more problems, learn more, and work more skillfully, but doubts about their expertise multiply along with these demands. As efforts to improve humanity have grown, so have our ambitions, our sophistication, and our critical capacities. Although better scientific and professional knowledge can inform practitioners' understanding and work, there is ample reason to doubt that this knowledge will end dispute or uncertainty. One reason is the idea of progress that these professions exemplify, for the more they prosper, the better we can see how much remains undone and what might have been better done. Such insights are a regular accompaniment of progress in human improvement.

I have mentioned only a few bits of evidence among many that might be marshaled on these points, but they are basic because they touch on the ends and means of improvement. Practitioners and commentators argue about whether such uncertainties and disputes are a temporary problem that will be eliminated with the progress of social science and professional knowledge or a permanent

feature of such work. They debate whether these professions are sciences, practical arts, or social engineering. Unlike carpentry or plumbing, the very nature of these professions and practitioners' knowledge and skills are matters of continuing uncertainty and often of ferocious dispute. Moreover, this account is only one source of uncertainty, for no practitioner can entirely anticipate how clients will respond in classes, therapy sessions, and other settings. Teachers are regularly surprised by students' interpretation of a story or their solution to a math problem and often must revise their approach in consequence. Human improvers cannot work without their clients, but work with them typically opens up uncertainty.

Practitioners' efforts to manage the paradox of expertise are complicated by a second predicament: they depend on clients. They can succeed only if their clients strive for and achieve success. If students, patients, and members of organizations do not become practitioners of their own improvement, professionals cannot succeed. A carpenter can produce results if he has the skills and knowledge of the trade, the will to work, and good materials, but all of a teacher's art and craft will be useless unless students embrace the purposes of instruction as their own and seek them with their own art and craft. This is one reason that students' resistance to teachers' direction can be a potent source of students' influence; it can be threatening not simply because students defy authority but also because they deny teachers success. Clients' will and capabilities are no less important than those of practitioners; indeed, practitioners' work in these trades often aims to cultivate their clients' will to better themselves and their skill at such work. Whatever their own attainments and position, workers depend on their less skilled, less mature, or less healthy clients for their own success and satisfaction.[6]

This is no theoretical matter, for human improvers and their clients often differ about their work. Teachers who are eager for Shakespeare or medieval history regularly encounter students who want accounting or auto mechanics. In such cases the purposes of instruction must be negotiated and renegotiated as part of instruction because clients' commitment is essential. Improvement cannot go forward without willing participants, but clients regularly fear improvement, doubt its possibility, are indifferent, or prefer something other than what practitioners offer.[7]

Practitioners' dependence is manifest everywhere in their work. It can affect the politics of practice, because practitioners cannot succeed without clients who work with them toward their success. Often they can influence clients' motivation, but not always, and in any case they cannot control it. Moreover, the social organization of work is a potent influence on clients' commitment. Teachers in many public schools try to find ways to "motivate" their students because they work in unselective institutions that students are compelled to attend. Teachers in many selective private schools often work with students who want to be there, in which case problems of motivation are less acute. Similarly, most psychiatrists and psychoanalysts in private practice typically select clients who wish to work with them and use that mutual choice and patients' payment to help mobilize patients' engagement. The mobilization of commitment is managed differently in various sectors of each occupation. Private practitioners who select clients who seek assistance and pay for it have a less acute problem than their colleagues who work in public facilities that compel or accept all comers. In the former case the social arrangements of work manage a great deal of clients' commitment for the private practitioners, while in the latter their publicly practicing colleagues must try to mobilize

and sustain clients' commitment despite the wish of many that they were somewhere else and were doing something else.

One device that practitioners use in this connection is to delegate responsibility to clients. Therapists often assign patients a key role in deciding what problems should be solved and when they have been solved. Organization consultants invite clients to decide on the goals they will seek and when they have been achieved. Teachers often try to anticipate what particular students will find appealing and to make suitable assignments, and they often negotiate the content of instruction with students.[8]

Practitioners' dependence imposes limits on skill and knowledge additional to those arising from limits on expertise. If a neurotic patient refuses to discuss his problems, the therapist's special expertise may be of little avail; if anything helps, it may be the little-skilled suggestion that therapy cannot proceed unless the patient cooperates, and the silence that can follow. If eight-year-olds reject their teacher's plan for a French lesson, no amount of instructional knowledge of French is likely to help. Unspecialized coaxing by the teacher, a stern admonition from a parent, or a trip to the principal may do the trick. In such cases and many others, practitioners' expertise is insufficient to produce results or even to get started.

Practitioners often must supplement their own expertise with clients' consent and with the knowledge and skills that clients bring to bear. Clients' commitment and knowledge are essential companions of practitioners' expertise and often a nearly complete substitute for it, as when students' engagement with a subject enables them to learn despite weak teaching. The need for supplements would exist even if all practitioners were exquisitely skillful, for teachers, psychotherapists, and organization developers work on other human be-

ings whose commitment to improvement is essential for the mere opportunity to practice, let alone for success. No amount of improvement in practitioners' knowledge and skills, marvelous though it might be, could supplant clients' commitment and the many essential but little-skilled things that practitioners or others do to mobilize and sustain it. Here again, the problem is managed differently in varied social arrangements of practice. Practitioners in private practice or very selective public settings can count on selectivity to help mobilize clients' will to improve, while their equally skillful colleagues in unselective settings often must labor to mobilize that commitment.

The third predicament is that practitioners are pulled in contrary directions as they try to manage their dependence. Because professional success depends on clients' improvement, there are powerful incentives to press for dramatic change, since the greater the client's accomplishment, the greater the practitioner's success. But human improvement can be both risky and difficult because more ambitious improvements are more difficult to achieve and pose greater risks of failure. Old ideas or habits must be revised or abandoned if clients are to change, whether in learning physics, improving emotional health, or increasing organizational effectiveness. If improvement works, it can be exhilarating, but it frequently is difficult; after all, the old ideas and habits often worked, however roughly, and it may not be easy to cast them aside. Clients also must acquire new skills, habits, understanding, or states of organization, which also can be difficult and risky; if they cannot change as much as they had hoped, perhaps they cannot become the person they wished to be or were told they should become. In a world that values human improvement as one of its most precious ambitions, such failures can weigh heavily.[9]

The more that workers seek ambitious success for their clients, the more likely they are to provoke resistance, precipitate failure, or both. Because changes that are risky and difficult for clients threaten practitioners' prospects, they have incentives to define improvement in such a way that clients will not resist or can easily accomplish it, for modest improvement may be better than resistance or failure. Teachers, therapists, and their colleagues in sister practices regularly worry about whether they should aim low in order to avoid the risk of total failure by clients and achieve at least some success for themselves, or aim high in order to gain great improvement for their clients and similar accomplishment for themselves. The problem has no lasting or generally satisfactory solution, but it must be managed somehow if work is to continue.[10]

These three predicaments are unique to human improvement. Teachers and organization consultants need the will to work in addition to their specialized knowledge and skills, and in that respect they are just like carpenters and architects. But carpenters and architects do not require the consent and commitment of their wood or designs. Only teachers and colleagues in related occupations require clients who bend their own will and intelligence to the work, along with practitioners. Workers in these occupations thus face another predicament that derives from a combination of the last two: they have special status, authority, and influence, and their clients often are seen as unskilled, deficient, or even pathological, but workers in these occupations are useless without their clients and often powerless with them. Patients who doze on the couch and students who read comic books or send text messages in class impede not only their own improvement but also practitioners' progress as professionals.

This last point implies that the predicaments operate jointly, because practitioners are regularly caught between their claims to

special knowledge and their dependence on clients. Their expertise is essential for access to clients, for their clients' trust, for fees or salaries, for social position, and for results. But practitioners' expertise always is insufficient, and they must rely on other resources or arrangements, supplementary to specialized knowledge and skills, to sustain their work. Some of the supplements belong to clients—their will to work and their knowledge and skills. Others belong to practitioners and include everything from the courage to face uncertainty to the generosity of spirit that enables one person to devote himself to help others. Some belong to both practitioners and clients—the capability to understand each other and to put oneself in the intellectual or emotional place of the other. Such empathy and mutual understanding are essential to our lives as social animals, but they have been investigated much more in sociobiology and anthropology than in practices of human improvement.[11] Improved knowledge and skill are sorely needed in teaching and its sister practices, but no matter how well educated and experienced they may be, workers need much more than specialized knowledge and skill to do good work.

It therefore seems fair to say that human improvement professions are impossible.[12] Teachers, therapists, and organizational consultants do not constantly tear their hair or weep and wail; they go to work every day like anyone else, and they cope with boredom in addition to the problems sketched here. But their work requires the management of unique and often-deep difficulties that have no entirely satisfactory solutions, and the solutions that workers do patch together regularly come unglued.[13] At the same time, to say that these predicaments must be managed is not to say that practitioners must deal with them constantly or attentively. For one thing, practitioners and clients themselves can regulate how much they need to attend to the problems discussed here. If

psychotherapists and patients use cognitive behavior therapy to induce weight loss or end smoking, they need not struggle with great uncertainty about the ends and means of improvement. In contrast, uncertainty and doubt will increase if they use traditional "insight" therapies to help patients understand why they overeat or smoke, decide what they can do about it, and then try to do it, for doubt and uncertainty are essential in these therapies.

Practitioners and clients can thus increase the risk and difficulty of their work by embracing relatively complex and ambiguous purposes and methods, or they can ease matters by adopting relatively clear and simple objectives and methods. They are not absolutely free agents, but they can regulate work together from the inside by choosing the ends they seek and the means they use. Such regulation is a central element in human improvement because it allows workers and clients to shape how large the predicaments of human improvement will loom, and what skills, knowledge, and other personal resources they must deploy.

Furthermore, workers and clients are not Robinson Crusoes and Fridays, parked on islands all their own. Their work also is regulated by society, economy, and culture. Some teachers work in institutions that admit only talented and commited students and dismiss them for poor performance; they are less likely to struggle with dependence on students than equally capable colleagues who work in drab public schools. Some teachers work in schools or societies that have a strong consensus about educational results; they are less likely to be plagued by uncertainty about the ends and means of schooling than equally able colleagues who work in schools or systems torn by persistent disputes about those matters. Social arrangements in these occupations sharpen the predicaments of improvement in some cases and blunt them in others. Variation in

these arrangements increases the probability that unusual expertise will be needed to get barely decent results in some cases, while fine results can be achieved with modest expertise in others.

To attend to the predicaments of human improvement thus is not to claim that all practitioners constantly worry about them. Attentive coping is not the only way in which these problems are managed. Workers and clients can diminish or increase the attention they give to these predicaments by internal regulation of their practice, and occupations and societies can do so by how they configure the social arrangements of practice. Much can be learned by figuring out why some workers and clients are little troubled by the predicaments sketched here, while others are plagued by them. The predicaments are distinctive to these occupations, but they are not always at the top of workers' minds. I propose them as a useful way to interpret work in these occupations, whatever workers may worry about.

My claim that these occupations are distinctive also is not a claim that they are unique, for human improvement bears remarkable similarities to other work. In the early years of the twenty-first century, many occupations can make some claim to human betterment, and most do. Social progress is an increasingly widely accepted value, and more and more occupations and enterprises explain and justify themselves with reference to it. Advertisers assert that they are improving our capacity to satisfy emotional needs. Managers claim that they are improving our capacity to be productive or to enjoy work. Soap manufacturers announce that their products "care" for our children. Whatever one thinks of these claims, only teachers, psychotherapists, and their colleagues work directly on other humans in order to improve their minds, skills, and organizations.

But someone may ask: what about many other occupations, ignored thus far, in which practitioners work directly on others? Cosmetics salesclerks work on their customers, surgeons work on their patients, human resource managers in large corporations work on their employees, and prison guards work on prisoners. Great promises for human improvement are regularly made for cosmetics, health care, management, and involuntary detention. Can one deny that these are also practitioners of human improvement?

Consider the improvements and how they are cultivated. Surgeons do not try to make their patients into apprentice surgeons, nor do salesmen try to improve their clients' capacity to sell vacuum cleaners or encyclopedias.[14] Some managers try to help subordinates become managers, but many do not. In occupations such as sales, physical medicine, and many branches of management, practitioners strive for distinctive results: items sold or manufactured, profits earned, bones and organs repaired, and the like. Improving clients' minds, souls, and knowledge is subsidiary at best and often is either irrelevant or merely decorative. In guarding prisons or other police work, workers typically are more custodians than meliorists; their assignment is to keep people away from trouble, not to improve their capabilities.[15]

In contrast, teachers can succeed only if they help students acquire some elements of their own special expertise: knowledge of a subject, skill in explaining it, strategies for solving problems, and the like. When classical psychotherapists succeed, they typically do so by helping their patients acquire elements of their own therapeutic expertise: insight into emotional problems, understanding their sources, skill in noticing symptoms, and a grasp of the barriers to improvement. Only teachers and workers in sister trades must help their clients to learn how to improve, for only in these

occupations must clients become apprentice practitioners in order for the workers to succeed.

Thus if there are elements of human improvement in many modern occupations, there also are important differences between human improvement practices and other occupations in which people are processed. But it would be unwise to draw hard-and-fast lines between these types of work, for the distinctions are contested within occupations. Some human resource managers in firms define their work in terms of profits made or units produced, but others define it to include understanding achieved, knowledge acquired, and capacities improved. Some prison managers define their work in custodial terms, but some do seek prisoners' rehabilitation; some prison guards act as though they were teachers, while others are brutal or indifferent.[16] And while some teachers act like prison guards, others seek intellectual liberation for their charges. The shape that these occupations take in any given case depends on organizational differences, clients' dispositions, and workers' preferences, among other things.

Another reason to eschew rigid distinctions is that occupations change over time. Physicians conventionally defined their work in terms of patients' physical health, and many still do, but increasingly they see that physical health can depend on how well patients understand their problems and how firmly they commit to the solutions; hence physicians work more and more on understanding and mutual commitment. Five or six centuries ago, what little schoolteaching there was dealt either with simple skills useful in commerce and administration or with otherworldly salvation. The problems of human improvement were not on anyone's plate because secular betterment was not a socially accepted enterprise. Human improvement occupations are an invention of the last several

centuries, the progeny of efforts to realize the idea of progress in social practices. One result has been the transformation of several ancient occupations. Pastoral work, which was focused on otherworldly salvation for centuries, has gradually been reoriented; pastors still offer guidance in matters beyond experience, but they borrow from social work, education, and psychotherapy so that even their otherworldly work now includes elements of secular human improvement.

The boundaries of human improvement professions also blur because these trades are not similarly constituted in all societies and often are contested within them. The speed of modernization varies among nations, as does enthusiasm for the doctrine of progress. Psychotherapy has been much more popular in America, with its established Protestant passion for self-improvement, than in the European countries in which it was invented. Teaching addresses a more limited range of purposes in Asian societies than in the United States, but even Americans disagree deeply about the extent to which it should attend to human improvement. Fundamentalists often see teaching in traditional terms and argue that it should orient students to salvation. Some reformers and practitioners think that teaching ought to be restricted to traditional academic matters and eschew broader improvement, but the ubiquity of human improvement also is evident here, for fundamentalists explain their view of school as an alternative to the broad aims of secular education that aims at improved self-esteem, sex education, and other things, along with academic matters.

These arguments will persist, waxing and waning with circumstances, but they all are variations on an essential modern theme: humanity's capacity to better self and society, to repair mind, soul, and organization with specialized knowledge and skills. It is un-

profitable to define these occupations tightly because history and social variation outgrow tidy boundaries. We can see that some practices of human improvement (teaching, psychotherapy, and organization development) are further down the modern road than others, at least in the United States, and so more clearly exhibit the distinctive predicaments of this most modern work. We can also see that the same practices seem to be moving in a similar direction in less modern societies, and we can imagine that this movement may become more pronounced in the future.

It would be surprising if the momentum of human improvement did not increase, pulling more occupations and enterprises into channels that others already have taken. In a few decades many salesclerks may become practitioners of retail therapy, using goods, services, and clinical insight in this cause. There already is evidence that consumers search for emotional improvement in the goods and services they purchase, and that many salespeople skillfully assist them. Although I can delineate the leading features of practices like teaching and psychotherapy today, it seems reasonable to expect that ambitions for human improvement will continue to grow tomorrow if we assume that there will be no convulsive rejection or collapse of modern civilization. This expansion will be difficult to avoid in a civilization that identifies progress so closely with increased technical mastery, personal comfort, and satisfaction of individual wants.[17] The boundaries of this new family of practices thus will probably remain indistinct and weakly defined, partly because they lie along an uneven and shifting frontier.

This account throws some additional light on my claim that human improvement occupations are impossible. Because they make great modern promises for secular betterment, they open up many great modern puzzles. Each occupation organizes these matters

differently because each employs a distinctive approach to setting and solving the problems. Classical psychotherapy is mostly centered on the discourses of emotional renewal and self-discovery; practitioners and clients focus on defining and solving problems by probing personal history, practicing new habits, or both. In contrast, teachers set and solve human improvement problems in the discourses associated with various academic subjects, theories of learning or schooling, or some combination of the two. But although the specific terms of reference vary from one human improvement occupation to another, these occupations still have much in common. Workers all try to better the human condition in some specific cases by increasing their clients' capacity to think, feel, or act. As a result, workers and clients are regularly confronted with certain common problems. What can this person become? How will we define human improvement in a given case? What methods of human betterment are best and most appropriate to achieve that progress? And how will we know if we have done well, or well enough, or whether we have done anything constructive at all? Should workers take an expansive view of human possibility and press for great improvement, or should they restrict their dependence and limit the demands on themselves and their clients by setting simpler and easier goals?

Workers in these remarkable trades thus face versions of the problems of producing and assessing human progress that all modern societies confront in national social policy. To undertake human improvement is to do the most essentially modern work. Because teachers, therapists, and organizational consultants try to deliver on these most distinctive promises of modern civilization, they also wrestle with the problems of defining and justifying human improvement with which entire societies have struggled throughout

the modern centuries. But they confront these problems in the midst of particular individual efforts to improve other human beings, rather than engaging them on the grand scale of social policy. As an analyst, I can make hay from the predicaments of human improvement, but practitioners must somehow find ways to manage them that are good enough to warrant work with the person in the next seat, the next hour, or the next consultation.

3

TEACHING

To teach is always to teach something. If we thought that a chef was instructing an apprentice, it would be because we observed the exchange of knowledge about cooking. If we saw them reading the newspaper or discussing baseball, we would doubt that there was instruction about cooking. Knowledge in transit is essential for teaching, a view that observers reflect when they describe situations in which there is none. Then they say that teachers seem to be "going through the motions" or doing "nonteaching."[1] The lack of knowledge in transit empties teaching of an essential ingredient.

But if knowledge in transit is a hallmark of teaching, how can one draw boundaries around the occupation? Teaching in schools and universities is only part of a vast array of activities in which humans transmit knowledge with the intent or effect of instruction. Parents do it with children, who regularly return the favor, as do plumbers with clients, priests with parishioners, officials with voters, and radio announcers with listeners. To note that instruction is everywhere is not to deny that it is one of humanity's most distinctive enterprises. The transmission of knowledge and skills is crucial to everything from housecleaning to high culture, but

most of this distinctive activity is carried on in quite ordinary channels. Deliberately practiced teaching is only one modest current in a great sea of informal and often unintended instruction.[2]

Is anyone who swims in that sea a teacher? From one angle this seems undeniable. We all can testify to learning from others who did not intend to teach us: were they not our teachers? We also may have taught when we least intended it and often least wished it; if it is called to our attention, we may be surprised or chagrined and deny an intent to instruct, but those who learned often insist that we taught them a great deal and are wounded by our denials. Can we reject their testimony?

We can, for teaching and learning are two distinct endeavors, sometimes connected, but often not. Much learning depends on no attentive teaching, and much attentive teaching produces no learning. Each of us offers many occasions for others to learn as we do things that include no attention to teaching them. We learn by imitating others in myriad ways, even adopting fragments of other people whom we admire or rejecting fragments that repel us. Such learning occurs in sibling differentiation, as brothers and sisters shape themselves in light of each other, embracing some attributes that they find attractive and rejecting others. Few siblings seem to teach this consciously, but many learn from example. It also occurs in what sociologists term peer influence, or context effects, as students in schools learn values and attitudes from each others' attention to athletics, or school work or dating. Sometimes these affect academic learning. We form sentiments and values similarly, learning from words or actions that were never intended to teach anything. Our learning does not mean that someone was teaching. If learning were possible only from attentive teaching, the transmission of knowledge would be terribly slow, and society would be much

more cumbersome than it is. One reason that society works is that humans learn a great deal by vicarious means. We observe others, we read, and we listen to radio or watch television. Although most action intends no tuition, we nonetheless learn from it.

Independent learning from unintended examples may seem sloppy to the scholastic mind, but there is much to recommend it. It greatly reduces the cost of transmitting knowledge and skills, so scarce time and intelligence can be allocated elsewhere. We could not turn inattentive tuition into deliberate instruction without forgoing much other social activity, because there simply is not enough time, money, or mind to deliberately teach everything that must or might be learned. Hence I distinguish teaching practice from the great sea of informal and ordinary instruction. This distinction has two elements: teaching practice is relatively deliberate and attentive, while ordinary tuition is casual and inattentive; and practicing teachers seek to connect their teaching with students' learning, while inattentive instructors give learning little or no heed. These two attributes are distinct, for teachers can easily attend closely to instruction while giving little or no thought to making connections with learning. In fact, many teachers do just that: they focus on the composition and content of lectures without attending either to what students will make of their speech or to how they might compose it to enhance students' understanding.

This implies a distinction between the occupation of teaching and teaching practice, for many who engage in the occupation do not cultivate a practice of teaching. Few commentators on teaching noticed this, but John Dewey did: "Teaching may be compared to selling commodities. We should ridicule a merchant who said that he had sold a great many goods although no one had bought any. But perhaps there are teachers who think that they have done

a good day's teaching irrespective of what students have learned. There is the same equation between teaching and learning that there is between selling and buying."[3]

Teaching practice thus is an artifice, an unnatural act, a contrived alternative to letting learners "pick it up on their own."[4] Practicing teachers seek to improve learning by organizing instruction that will guide, harness, and support it; it depends, among other things, on the mutual understanding to which I referred in the previous chapter. In such work teachers take responsibility for students' learning; they give close attention to learners' thinking and to designing instruction to advance it. Such teaching is responsive to learning, as well as responsible to the subject matter. In ordinary instruction, teaching and learning connect only in unintended collisions, unknowing coexistence, or casual and fleeting contacts, and there is little or no evidence of the teacher's effort to read the other person's mind. Learners can profit from such encounters if they appropriate the opportunities that others unknowingly present, but in such cases success in learning is not the fruit of successful teaching. To take responsibility for students' learning is not to imply that teachers can learn for students; only students can learn. It does imply that teachers cultivate practices that are most likely to enable students to learn.[5]

Of course most teachers believe both that they intend students to learn, and that their teaching is intended to accomplish that. Yet their instruction is marked by little close attention to learners' thinking and little effort to design instruction to advance it. Such teachers make few efforts to put themselves in the learner's intellectual shoes with respect to the material in question, and make few efforts to teach in light of that knowledge. If teaching and learning connect in such cases it is because learners are able to make use

of instruction despite teachers' inattention to how they think and what they make of the work; they appropriate the opportunities that teachers present, but their learning is not the fruit of teaching practice.

There can be no absolute distinction between teaching practice and ordinary and conventional instruction. There are shreds of attention in much seemingly automatic behavior, and great patches of automatic behavior underlie attentive action. But the amount of attention and the intensity of efforts to link teaching and learning vary greatly. At one extreme are actions that embody no intention to instruct, no effort to make connections with learning, and no effort by the "teacher" to understand a learner's work, while at the other are deliberately cultivated teaching practices that are informed by carefully thought-out intentions and actions designed to encourage learning. In the very large middle is teaching which seems natural and sensible in part because it is conventional, but which lacks much deliberately cultivated teaching practice. The more attentive teaching is, and the more it seeks connections with learning, the more it merits the appellation of teaching practice.

Attentive and Inattentive Teaching

Many apprentices learn their trades with little benefit from attentive instruction. They work with journeymen who have no scheme for teaching save, perhaps, "Watch me," "Do what I do," or "Do what I tell you and don't bother me with questions." In such cases novices learn "from experience." The journeymen may correct the novices' mistakes, they may only growl or shout in irritation, they may reissue the orders, or they may simply brush the apprentices aside and redo the offending work themselves. This sort of learning

is as common in play as it is at work. Many weekend sailors learn from inattentive teaching as their skipper uses them as a crew, ordering sheets loosened on some points of a sail and trimmed on others. The weekenders must learn a few things, for example, that they are to pull the sheets taut and cleat them fast when sailing upwind and loosen them when sailing off the wind. Both are important bits of knowledge in sailing, and both must be learned by anyone who intends to sail. But as in many apprenticeships, the weekenders learn by imitating actions that have little instructional design.

These journeymen and skippers are teachers, if by that term we mean someone who presents opportunities from which others might learn. But then we all are teachers all the time that we are awake and in human company. Such casual teachers are sometimes attentive in the sense that they know that novices can learn by imitation, by following orders, and by making sense of things themselves. Sometimes they intend that novices learn that way. But that approach does not add up to a practice of teaching, for one finds little or no added element of attentive instruction beyond the knowledge that learning may occur. These journeymen and sailors do not demonstrate the things to be learned; they do not present or re-present the elements of their work in ways that make them available to novices, nor do they create opportunities for novices to apprehend and try out what they are to learn. They do not attempt to put themselves in the learners' place and frame their own actions accordingly. Instead of being offered tuition in how to perform the desired acts, novices are simply told to pull on that sheet or solder that joint. To do otherwise would require the creation of conditions in which teaching counts along with plumbing or sailing, but if all attention is given to plumbing or sailing, there is little or no room to explain why these things must be done, or must be done one way and not

another, let alone for journeymen to select examples, demonstrate the work, and offer opportunities for practice. Practitioners simply drag novices along in their wake and let them keep up as best they can. We regularly learn from such opportunities by a combination of imitation, blindly following orders, noticing the consequences of our actions, and figuring things out for ourselves. Such learning is common, unavoidable, and often fruitful. It can be challenging and quite enjoyable. In Mark Twain's account of how he learned to become a Mississippi River boat pilot, he celebrated Mr. Bixby, his master, arguing (despite much evidence to the contrary) that he was not a teacher.[6] But when novices learn in these ways, it is not because someone else has thoughtfully organized occasions for them to do so.[7]

Attentive instruction spreads out in degrees from this emaciated extreme. Some journeymen cultivate a spare practice of teaching: they issue orders, provide an occasional example, and offer novices opportunities to practice alone. Then they wait. Those who get it right are given another order or example. Those who do not may be given more time, but often instruction ends there. Such teaching is considered, but austere. Guidance for learning is carefully rationed.

Other journeymen add a few demonstrations to such work. Carpenters may teach apprentices the use of handsaws by demonstrating how to cross-cut a two-by-four cleanly. They show how to grip the handle, the length of the stroke, and where to bear down, but beyond such demonstrations they offer little instruction. Having been "shown," apprentices must learn the rest on their own, by trial and error, recalling the demonstration and watching. Some journeymen do more. They explain what they do while they are doing the work. When the novice begins, the carpenter holds the saw over her shoulder and guides the apprentice's movement so she can get the

feel of a proper stroke. Then the carpenter watches the novice practice and comments, coaches, questions, and demonstrates. If the novice is puzzled, the carpenter answers questions, revises tasks, offers another example, or returns to earlier material.

There is enormous variation in the extent of attentive teaching within any occupation. Some carpenters and plumbers give little or no time to their apprentices' learning, while others devise many opportunities for them to watch, practice, correct, and question. Such variation is no less apparent in schools than in carpentry or plumbing. Some teachers attend closely to their demonstrations and discussions with students and consider and reconsider instruction in much detail, but others give little or no time to such matters. Instead, they read from texts that others wrote and never consider the argument, the examples, or how they convey the material. Or they routinely follow prescriptions handed down by higher authorities and never consider the content, its relation to the knowledge field in question, or how they elucidate it. These people work in an occupation called teaching, so we call them teachers, but we could not fairly say that they cultivate a practice of teaching; they are the classroom equivalent of plumbers who use apprentices with no attention to teaching, and who give little attention to apprentices' questions and offer few explanations.

Hence it seems reasonable to say that teaching practice is not the same thing as the occupation of teaching. From one perspective, teaching practice is only a subset of that occupation, for many teachers' work is informed by little conscious attention to linking teaching with learning. Of course, many teachers who work attentively some of the time teach mechanically on other occasions. Cultivating a practice of teaching is only part of what members of this occupation do, and often a very small part.

But the practice of teaching also is broader than the occupation because people who stand in front of classes and are called teachers are not the only source of attentive instruction. Written materials, videotapes, and computer programs are other sources, as are learners' friends if they work together. Agents of attentive instruction have multiplied in the past two centuries as informal social arrangements for education have been replaced by formal educational agencies, and as new instructional media and technologies have been invented, developed, and widely adopted.

To say that deliberate instruction has grown in specialized settings thus does not necessarily mean that it has shrunk in ordinary life, for there are signs of more deliberation there as well. For instance, the child-rearing practices of cosmopolitan middle- and upper-middle-class parents are almost certainly more deliberately instructional now than two or three centuries ago. Though children in such homes may get more deliberate teaching at school than their counterparts did in the seventeenth century, it seems likely that many of them also have more instructional opportunities at home. A similar phenomenon can be observed in some occupations. Commercial employees in the seventeenth century learned a great deal on the job, and they certainly attended school less than their counterparts today. But some of this work has grown more complex, with new technology and organizational change, and some work has grown more humane. In such cases both the need and opportunities for deliberate instruction of workers increased. But there are many other occupations in which changes in technology and organization have reduced the scope of worker skills, and thus the possibilities for deliberate instruction on the job. Deliberate teaching in formal agencies of instruction probably has not grown at the expense of informal instruction.

Thus there is much more attentive classroom teaching now than ever before, thanks to the spread of schooling, but such teaching is probably a decreasing fraction of all deliberate instruction because of the rise of new technologies and forms of social relations. That fraction seems likely to diminish further as the media of instruction and communication multiply, and as sophisticated television and computer-video systems take a growing share of instruction. The social organization of teaching as a specialized occupation in schools has helped support increasing attentiveness in teaching, but that occupation is only one of an increasing number of platforms that support attentive instruction. Teaching practice is less and less the preserve of people who preside over classes in schools and universities.

Connections between Teaching and Learning

Teaching practice includes conscious efforts to make connections with learning in order to advance it. Wherever practicing teachers work and however fleetingly, they try to bridge the chasms that often yawn between teaching and learning. Deliberately seeking to make such connections is a crucial and even constitutive feature of teaching practice, and it depends, among many other things, on the mutual mind reading that sociobiologists and anthropologists argue was essential to the evolution of our species. If teachers cannot somehow improve learning over what would occur in conventional, informal, or casual instruction, it is difficult to see what claim they might have to cultivate a practice of instruction.

I will discuss how teachers can make connections that promote learning, but those connections are not made just anywhere. People make many connections in bars and on beaches, and teaching

and learning often ensue, but bars and beaches are not distinctive terrains of teaching. In order to discuss how teachers make connections that promote learning, one must discern the terrains in which teachers and learners meet. They must be terrains that include attentive and conventional instruction, whether they occur in classrooms or in computer environments. I have been able to identify three. One is the knowledge that teachers extend to learners, and how they extend it. The second is the organization of instructional discourse. The third is teachers' acquaintance with students' knowledge. These three terrains do not name "essential" or "generic" skills and knowledge. They are common to and required for all sorts of instruction, but teachers' work in each is realized in many different ways. There may be others than these three; I do not claim that this list is exhaustive, though I have been unable to add to it. It is sufficient for my purposes that the three cover much of the ground. To the extent that one teaches or constructs a practice of teaching, one does so in those terrains, whatever the matter to be taught and learned and wherever teachers and learners meet.

Knowledge is one of the terrains in which teaching and learning can be linked. Teachers of all sorts somehow frame what is to be learned and give it some focus and definition, even if they only assign chapters from a book and tell students to read them. They compose knowledge for learners even if they only identify a sequence of steps, a body of material, or a method of study. In these ways and others, teachers extend knowledge to students and offer connections that are intended to advance learning. This knowledge can include standard texts, computer-based problem sets, and carefully organized "experience." Despite the differences, all this knowledge is devised or appropriated in order to guide and support learning. Hence it depends on some anticipation of what learners are likely to

know already, and on what the most fruitful ways to frame and extend knowledge may be, even if these are only the most routine and unexamined assumptions.

But knowledge is as supple as putty. It can be extended in ways that limit and simplify the connections between teaching and learning or that deepen and complicate those connections. Some teachers construe knowledge as inert and finished: teachers tell facts and procedures, and students practice and remember them. Such work can be quite attentive and deliberate, as in the "effective teaching" that came into vogue in the United States in the 1970s and 1980s, or it can be quite inattentive, as in much routine instruction. I will argue in the next chapter that this sort of knowledge extension is conventional, a sort of default, and it has come to seem "natural." But whether the teaching is attentive or not, this is only one way to construe knowledge. Some other teachers construe it as the result of a practice of inquiry: to know is to be a competent inquirer, to frame problems fruitfully, to make disciplined arguments, and to interpret material and defend results convincingly. The different conceptions of knowledge—ideal types to be sure, but useful contrasts—have large consequences for how connections can be made between teaching and learning. The more constrained and mechanical the teachers' treatment of knowledge, the simpler the intellectual connections that teachers and students make, and the more discrete each connection seems. When teachers and students construe knowledge in this way, they can relatively easily make direct connections, even if they are often superficial. In contrast, the more expansive and flexible the treatment of knowledge, the more complex each connection is, and the less discrete it seems. When teachers and learners construe knowledge in this fashion, the intellectual connections they seek are more complex and less

direct. Such connections can grow rich and deep, but they are relatively difficult to make. Mutual understanding is easier in the first case than in the second, in part because the cognitive operations are less complex and partly because uncertainty is therefore more limited. Knowledge is a crucial medium for regulating the connections between teaching and learning, but the nature of those connections varies with how knowledge is construed and extended.

Knowledge cannot be extended in a vacuum. A social organization of discourse is required, even if it is only one teacher and one student, and it is the second terrain in which teachers and learners work. Some discourses are face-to-face, while others are indirect, as with correspondence courses and television, radio, or computer networks. There also is wide variation even among those who work face-to-face: some work in large lectures in which teachers monopolize the discourse, while others work in small groups in which conversation flows from all sides.

Discourse organization counts because it structures the possible connections between teaching and learning, and thereby shapes the nature and extent of knowledge exchange and opportunities for mutual understanding. Some kinds of discourse organization multiply the opportunities for learners to participate actively, to exchange knowledge, and thus to influence instruction, while others constrain those opportunities. Many teachers and students work in correspondence colleges or pure lectures, in which teachers broadcast assignments in writing or voice, students write responses, and teachers read them and perhaps comment. Teachers and students rarely or never meet. They exchange monologues at a distance, and this solitary discourse limits the range and depth of possible connections. Students rarely or never see one another's work, let alone exchange ideas about it, so opportunities for mu-

tual understanding are limited. The fewer such opportunities, the less likely learners are to learn from one another, as well as from a teacher.

In contrast, some students and teachers devise discourses that allow them to exchange knowledge in extended interactions. That can occur not only in small seminars but also can be contrived in lectures, and it occurs increasingly in computer environments. Whatever the medium, these conversations offer a greater range of knowledge and interpretation than most lectures or correspondence courses, so there can be more opportunities for students to scrutinize their own formulations in light of others'. In such cases each student's learning is more likely to be shaped by others' contributions, as well as by her encounter with course materials. As in correspondence courses or lectures, teachers make assignments, students write, and teachers read and return the writing with comments, but unlike most correspondence courses and lectures, such conversations may increase opportunities to exchange knowledge. When teachers work in a richer and more diverse discourse, they have more opportunities to extend knowledge to students and can help students extend it.

Some discourse organizations offer many chances to connect teaching and learning, while others reduce those chances. But discourse organization affects only opportunities for knowledge exchange; teachers and students must shape and use the discourse to take advantage of and sustain those opportunities. The form of discourse is not controlling. Some teachers who work in distance education devise ways to push the organization's limits so that relatively rich exchanges occur; other teachers turn small seminars into rigid recitations that limit knowledge exchange. But teachers and students have more opportunities to exchange knowledge and

learn how each other thinks in some discourse organizations than others; if they shape those discourses so as to capitalize on the opportunities that they offer, they enrich and complicate their work. Yet, as the possible connections are multiplied, so are the demands, on both students and teachers, of creating and sustaining a complex discourse because there is much more for each mind to apprehend and make sense of, and thus much more to mutually understand. Because such work requires knowledge and skill well beyond conventional teaching, it seems fair to label it unnatural. In contrast, when teachers and students use discourse organizations that constrain connections between teaching and learning, they reduce the demands of their work, in part because there is much less for each mind to apprehend, make sense of, and mutually understand. Teachers who broadcast ideas in lectures or correspondence courses need only speak or write, and they may take few opportunities to probe students' knowledge. For their part, students need only read or listen, take notes, or send someone with a recorder.

Teachers' acquaintance with students' knowledge is the third terrain in which learning and teaching may connect. All teachers must adopt some stance toward acquainting themselves with students' knowledge, but teachers and students have immense flexibility to regulate others' access to their knowledge. Teachers can inquire deeply into students' knowledge and adjust instruction accordingly, or they can ignore what students know and adjust instruction not at all.[8] Students can disclose their ideas freely, carefully ration them, or resist any disclosure. Additionally, teachers can inquire into students' knowledge in many ways. They can ignore what their students say in favor of reading about children and discussing them with faculty colleagues, or they can directly attend to students' work. Even those who attend directly can do so in

a great variety of ways. They can focus on theories of learning or attend to what learners actually make of their assignments. They can attend regularly and extensively or only infrequently. And even those who attend regularly can attend only to evidence of congruence between their teaching and students' knowledge rather than search more broadly for signs of minds at work. Relatively few teachers search more broadly because doing so requires that they step a bit outside their own thought worlds, learn how to explore students' knowledge and ideas from other perspectives, and seek ways to connect students' ideas with the material under consideration. Teaching of this sort requires an unusually complex, sophisticated, and demanding sort of mind reading and for that reason it also can fairly be termed unnatural.

Teachers who acquaint themselves deeply with students' knowledge open up many opportunities to make connections with learning. Doing so can be useful, but it also can be difficult because it multiplies the signals they must monitor and the evidence to which they must attend. It also can be humbling or painful because such work often multiplies the chances to notice missing connections, different interpretations, and confusions. Teachers who cast a wide net into students' knowledge increase the connections that they can make with learning, but they also multiply the difficulties that they turn up. But teachers who attend only a little or narrowly to students' knowledge constrain their opportunities to make intellectual connections that may advance learning, and so they minimize evidence of trouble. Hearing little or nothing from students, they observe few missing connections, few differing interpretations, and few confusions. Similarly, teachers who search only for congruence between students' knowledge and their own limit the sort of signals they need to monitor. They also limit the domain in which connections with

learning can be made, and simplify the work of making those connections. There are costs to such conventional or natural work, but also benefits.

These are the terrains in which attentive teaching can occur: knowledge and how it is extended, the organization of instructional discourse, and acquaintance with students' knowledge. Each offers a great range of ways to connect teaching and learning, and hence each entails a corresponding range of teachers' expertise. If elementary-school teachers construe and extend knowledge in routine and algorithmic ways, they need do relatively little to connect teaching and learning (i.e., they write problems on the board and tell students to practice them). Teachers also need modest skills of explanation and demonstration—the capacity to write things on the board, to repeat them, to detect deviations from prescribed procedures, and the like. In contrast, if teachers construe knowledge and its extension as the outcomes of practices of inquiry, they must do much more to connect teaching and learning. They must unpack the problems they present, offering them in different forms and from different angles, because these are likely to offer students opportunities to connect with the ideas. To do that teachers require complex skills of explanation and demonstration—the capacity to represent the same idea in different ways, the knowledge to discriminate between key ideas and mere procedures, and more. In these ways and others they represent academic material in ways that are likely to be more responsive to learners, and thus responsible. Teachers can work attentively in either mode, but the nature of teaching differs greatly between the two cases, as do the intellectual demands on teachers and students. Teaching and learning can connect in both cases, but quite differently.

The sorts of knowledge and skills required to connect teaching and learning also vary greatly among the three domains. For in-

stance, to organize and sustain a complex instructional discourse, teachers must be able to manage social interactions, but in order to extend knowledge as the outcome of a practice of inquiry, they must understand the material, have intellectual imagination, and the like. Knowledge can be elegantly extended by writing lessons, textbooks, or computer programs from a closet, but the skill to manage social interaction can neither be acquired nor exercised in such a place. Yet teachers who know little of a subject may be adept managers of social interaction.

Because of these differences, each terrain of teachers' knowledge and skills is at least partly independent of the others, in the sense that the knowledge, skills, and other resources required to work in one are at least partly distinct, analytically and practically, from the knowledge and skills required to work in others. Teachers' work in one terrain often depends little on work in another. Many teachers who view knowledge as the result of learners' inquiry nonetheless monopolize instructional discourse and restrict students' opportunities to inquire to the privacy of their minds. Although these teachers may speak and write as "constructivists," they act as though they could construct students' understanding for them. Teachers can be quite sophisticated and expert in one terrain and quite primitive in another. They can cultivate a highly developed practice of teaching in one terrain while maintaining an almost entirely inattentive practice of teaching in another. But teachers cannot work only in one terrain; though I treat them separately for purposes of analysis, when I teach I must work in all three.

Hence the knowledge and skills of teaching are open to a blinding variety of constructions. Lee Shulman devised the term "pedagogical content knowledge," to refer, roughly speaking, to the knowledge and skill that enables teachers to make knowledge of material accessible to students.[9] Some researchers write as though

pedagogical content knowledge were a fixed domain that could be identified, studied, and transmitted to intending teachers, but in fact it is a vast set of possibilities. Depending on how teachers and students construe their work together, pedagogical content knowledge can take very different and even radically opposed forms. It is not a body of knowledge, but a category that refers to many different and often divergent bodies of knowledge and skill; they all refer to pedagogy, but because pedagogy can vary so greatly, they do not necessarily refer to the same pedagogy.

It follows that the demands on teachers and learners vary enormously depending on how they work in the three terrains. One set of demands is intellectual. Teachers who seek rich and deep connections between teaching and learning incur large demands for themselves and their students, if learners accept them. Few students understand a subject simply because their teacher gives a lecture or assigns reading; most need help if they are to understand, let alone understand deeply. They need explanation, demonstration, and opportunities to practice what they are learning. They need help in trying out and revising their formulations, chances to try again, and opportunities to apply what they learn in new situations. Teaching that affords these opportunities requires extensive knowledge and skills; teachers must know the material deeply, they must know how to bring that knowledge usefully to bear in instruction, and they must know how to help students learn how to do the work, no small matter in itself. Such work can be quite demanding for teachers and learners.

In teaching multiplication, for instance, teachers who work in this way may try to unpack the mathematical ideas, representing them in different ways. They may show that 12 × 12 can be understood as repeated addition (i.e., twelve added twelve times), or as the combina-

tion of equal groups ($y \times 12$). Or they may represent these ideas more concretely, by combining equally numbered groups of blocks, apples, or jars of beans on a table, or in pictures on the board. But in all of these cases, the teachers try to help students construct a sense of the operations and the mathematical meanings that underlie the conventional algorithm: $12 \times 12 = 144$. Teachers do this by presenting the ideas and operations in many different ways. In their search for ways to cultivate students' understanding, some teachers even invite students to devise representations themselves, and explain them to each other. Their premise is that articulating the ideas will help students to get a grip on them. But when teachers do such things they are drawn from helping students to understand mathematical procedures into elucidating the nature of mathematical arguments. For in order to reason well about how to represent the mathematical relationships in multiplication students must be able to distinguish between representations that make mathematical sense in the situation—for instance, twelve jars of twelve beans each—and those that do not make as much sense, such as twelve jars of ten beans each, and one jar of 24 beans. To teach and learn multiplication in this way therefore is not just to probe why certain procedures make sense, but also to explore the differences between more and less defensible mathematical reasoning. Hence this approach to teaching multiplication raises questions about how mathematicians explain and justify their reasoning, no mean issue. Discussion of it is not one ordinarily associated with teaching fourth grade arithmetic—or college calculus, for that matter. Though such unnatural work can be quite rewarding it also is demanding, in part because it rests on teachers' ethical commitment to take responsibility for learning.

Teachers who seek simpler and less deep connections with learning limit the demands on themselves and their students. They can

copy material on the board and show students mechanically how to remember dates or work problems. Teachers need only to remember facts and procedures, present them in a usable order, demonstrate their use, and perhaps offer useful mnemonic devices. They also must be able to distinguish correct from incorrect answers. But none of these require great intellectual skill nor deep knowledge of a subject, though many professors who teach in this way reveal great skill and deep knowledge in their own research, writing, and conversations with colleagues.

This sketch of my analysis provides a frame with which to distinguish the elements of quality in teaching. It also helps to illuminate the connections between the analysis of teaching and the problems of human improvement discussed in Chapter 2. If teachers present knowledge as facts and procedures, they constrain uncertainty; they deal only with right and wrong answers and correct and incorrect procedures. Ambiguity about what students and teachers know, or how well they know it, or what knowledge is, is constrained. An observer might say that the foundations of knowledge remain mysterious and confusing in this case, but in practice knowledge seems crisp and sure; teachers and students can quickly tell right answers from wrong ones. To adopt simpler and more mechanical views of knowledge seems to clarify the purposes of teaching and learning and thereby constrain uncertainty about the work. Students need not think deeply, need not justify and explain their work, and need not understand deeply. The problems of human improvement are limited.

But when teachers treat knowledge as the outcome of a practice of inquiry, they open up uncertainty. If mathematics and literature are defined in broad and ambitious terms, one finds that there are several plausible answers to many questions and several plau-

sible paths to an answer. That magnifies ambiguity about what knowledge is, about what one knows, and when one knows it well, or well enough. Such uncertainty is essential to deep understanding, but it increases the difficulty and risks of instruction because students and teachers must operate in a less clearly defined terrain and produce much more complex performances. It can be unclear what the answers are, or what is correct. Students have many more things to learn, and they must work harder to learn them. In addition to grasping complex ideas instead of facts and rules, students must learn to live with intellectual uncertainty and make disciplined use of it. Teachers cannot navigate such terrain well without a deep knowledge of the material and a broad range of perspectives on it. They must be able to find many ways through the material and to shift direction rapidly. The intelligent management of uncertainty plays a large part in such work, and the predicaments of human improvement—dependence on students and uncertainty about success—are more vividly present and difficult to manage. Given decades of research on the mind's aversion to uncertainty, it seems fair to term such work unnatural.

Teachers may choose between these approaches attentively or not, and they may choose them easily or at great cost. But in any case the ways in which teachers work affect their management of the predicaments of human improvement. I may distinguish the two levels of problem solving for ease of analysis, but they are not distinct in practice. In some other world, in which students learned to reason about mathematics or literature at their parents' knees, some of these difficulties would be eased. But in America in the first years of the twenty-first century, the uncertainties of ambitious teaching often baffle and confuse teachers and learners. They worry about whether they can teach or learn such stuff, or they fret about the

ambiguity of lessons. They wonder how they could teach in such ways when they are judged by students' standardized test scores. For these reasons and others, they often stick with facts and rules.

However teachers solve these problems, they find that skills and knowledge are never enough. Those who seek deep and rich connections with learning also must have a taste for intellectual adventure, a tolerance for differing views, the patience to explore unusual ideas, courage to probe the unknown, and the strength of character to support others who are less experienced as they try to acquire these qualities. They must cultivate mutual understanding in themselves and their students, as well as the intellectual perceptiveness that sustains such work. Extraordinary knowledge and skills are essential if teachers wish to make deep and rich connections with learning, but they are usable only when they are accompanied by many supplements and alternatives. Indeed, the more skillful and knowledgeable the practice that teachers try to construct, the greater the range and subtlety of supplements to knowledge and skills that they require. Conversely, when teachers work in less expert ways, they constrain the range and subtlety of supplements to expertise that they must put into play.

One theme in this discussion is that teaching can be realized in an astonishing variety of ways. To put this another way, teachers can invest their personal resources—their knowledge, skills, and supplements thereto—in remarkably varied ways. Many conserve those resources, for instance, by limiting their attention to students' knowledge; others conserve their resources by doing ambitious work in only one terrain of practice, although some work ambitiously in two or three. Teachers must work in all terrains si-

multaneously in order to teach, but the same teacher can work quite differently in one than she does in another at the same time. The possible combinations within and across the three terrains offer an amazing array of ways to teach. Teaching is supple: although individual teachers may be rigidly attached to their habits of work, there are immense opportunities for variation and internal adjustments within and among teachers.

My point is not that teachers are calculating, rational actors, carefully weighing the costs and benefits of every classroom move. Although some teachers seem quite attentive to such matters, others seem relatively unaware. My conjecture is interpretive: whatever teachers' awareness, teaching can be read as I propose. I seek to map the terrain of teaching and teaching practice, not to attribute motives. In the chapters that follow, I explore the sorts of performances that teaching and teaching practice can comprise, and the varied resources, social and individual, that those performances require. In doing so, I use three terms—ambitious teaching, attentive teaching, and responsible teaching—as synonyms of "teaching practice" to avoid monotonous repetition. All three terms refer to work with students that is intellectually demanding, attentive to students' work, conducted in thoughtful conversation, and thus usually requires considerable training.

I focus on the social resources of teaching in Chapter 4. I offer an overview of all those resources, but I consider in some detail how selectivity and social conventions about results can support or impede efforts to enact a practice of teaching. In Chapters 5, 6, and 7, I consider the three terrains of teaching and teaching practice discussed earlier in this chapter and the ways in which teachers' individual resources—knowledge, know-how, courage, and others—interact with social resources. Of course, rigid distinctions between

individual and social phenomena are implausible: we can mobilize courage and know-how only in and through social organization, and organizations are crippled if they lack skilled and knowledgeable individuals. But I use the distinction to explore just such interactions, and, as distinctions go, this ancient one has much to recommend it.

4

THE SOCIAL RESOURCES OF TEACHING

Teaching is typically seen as the work of an individual, but it is thoroughly social. One reason is that individual work requires social resources, including norms of appropriate work, the knowledge and know-how required to do the work, and standards of quality. Occupations cannot practice—only individuals or groups of individuals can do that—but those individuals cannot work without the specialized knowledge, skills, and common vocabularies that occupations foster and collect, the education, structured at least in part by the occupation, that prepares workers to practice, and standards for work that occupations help set. Some version of these social resources exists for any skilled occupation; I group them as infrastructure because they are the frame around which skilled work is built.

Another respect in which human improvement is social is that like all occupations, it is enmeshed in society and influenced by it. Doctors who work amid great poverty face somewhat different problems, and their patients typically have less success, than equally capable doctors who work in privileged communities. Teachers and students who work amid intense conflict about the ends and means of schooling are likely to have more difficulty settling on and succeeding at a

coherent course of study than similarly capable teachers and students who work with strong agreement about the ends and means of schooling. Those and other social conditions are social resources of an occupation, but as the examples suggest, resources can enable or impede work.

Human improvement is social in a third and more unique respect: workers labor on and with other people. One consequence is that social conditions such as conflict about the ends and means of work affect clients no less than workers, and the effects on clients often react on practitioners and vice versa. The social conditions that we think of as outside practice are active in what we think of as inside practice.

A second consequence is that those who work in human improvement cannot practice without their clients' will, skill, and commitment. Clients and practitioners seek honesty in organizations, understanding in learners, and emotional health in troubled individuals, among other things. Appreciable progress toward those results requires sustained and often-difficult work, and practitioners can achieve those results only by helping clients realize them in themselves. Teachers cannot "learn" students. Students depend on teachers for help, but teachers' success depends on students' learning. Each is the other's path to success, so good work requires unusual commitment to the work, to each other, and to each other's success. Mutual commitment to improvement is a crucial social resource and a constitutive element of good work in these occupations.

That commitment is influenced partly by individuals' capability and partly by the social settings of practice. One feature of those settings is social agreement about results. Agreement can make it easier to mobilize mutual commitment, while conflict about results can make it more difficult. Another feature is the locus of re-

sponsibility for results. If clients and practitioners share responsibility, mutual commitment to ambitious work is less difficult to mobilize than it is if workers or clients alone are responsible. Buy-in is another important feature of the social settings of work: if practitioners' work with clients results from mutual choice, a shared commitment to improvement is more likely to thrive than it is if their work together is not chosen or is compelled. Buy-in can be influenced by practitioners' skill at engaging clients and clients' engagement, but it also is shaped by how organizations manage clients' acceptance to and enrollment in practice.

A third consequence of improvers' work on and with other people is that the work itself is social. Teaching consists largely in the mobilization and use of social resources. Of course, students and teachers bring individual resources to the work, but those resources become active in instruction only when they are socialized—that is, when they are made part of the interaction among students or between students and a teacher. What teachers and students do together can be more or less than their individual resources might permit, depending on the interaction. Teaching consists not in what teachers know, but in what they know how to do with students and what students know how to do themselves, with one another, with some content, and with their teachers in their environment.[1]

The socialization of instructional resources can be illustrated in each of the three domains of teaching that I sketched in Chapter 3. First, teachers' knowledge becomes an instructional resource only if teachers make it available to students, which depends on how effectively they transform knowledge of history or mathematics into assignments, materials, conversation, and assessment. When it is effective, those transformations turn teachers' and students' knowledge and skills into social resources. Making knowledge available

requires not only knowledge of the subject but also the know-how to set academic tasks that will enable students to become novice practitioners of mathematics or history and thereby make knowledge their own. Responsible teaching also requires the ability to "read students' minds," that is, to understand how they think about academic subjects and the know-how to organize academic work accordingly. Students' knowledge also can become a social resource in instruction, as opposed to a resource for their own learning, to the extent that they make it accessible to other students, the teacher, or both. That, in turn, depends partly on how well they have learned to listen to teachers and fellow students, and partly on how well they have learned to explain themselves and to share their ideas with others.

Even if teachers effectively extend knowledge to students, it may not be used well; that depends on two other matters. One is how teachers and learners organize instructional discourse. Although that discourse is unavoidably social, teachers and learners can organize it to expand or contract social resources. They can organize discourse in ways that create opportunities to make knowledge more broadly available for exploration, interrogation, and application, thus creating opportunities for students and teachers to put themselves in each other's academic shoes and thereby better understand the material. Discourse organization of this sort makes it possible for students' knowledge to become a social resource of instruction, as opposed to a resource for their own learning, because the discourse encourages students to share knowledge. That also depends on how well they have learned to listen to teachers and fellow students, on how well they have learned to explain themselves, and how able they are to share their ideas with others. Alternatively, discourse can be organized in ways

that limit those opportunities. The more such opportunities are opened, the more social resources of instruction can be created. But creating such opportunities does not mean that they will be used well. That depends in part on the prior point—how capable teachers are at extending knowledge to students, and how capable students are at explaining themselves and understanding teachers and one another.

The creation and use of social resources also depend on how effectively teachers acquaint themselves with students' knowledge, and how effectively students make their knowledge available to teachers and one another. Knowledge extension and instructional discourse are both shaped by how well teachers can probe students' work and understanding. This acquaintance is social in the sense that it can occur only in social interaction and in the sense that, once acquired, it can become a social resource of instruction, because the more teachers are acquainted with students' knowledge, the more they can use it in instruction. But teachers can severely limit their acquaintance with students' knowledge by lecturing all the time, by calling on a few students a bit of the time, by searching only for the right answer and dismissing all other answers, or other such means. Students can limit teachers' acquaintance with their knowledge by speaking little or not at all, by not doing written work, by reading comics behind their schoolbooks, or by sending text messages. The more opportunities there are for teachers to acquaint themselves with students' knowledge and for students to share their knowledge, the more social resources of instruction can be created. Yet, creating such opportunities does not mean that they will be used well; that depends in part on the prior points: how capable teachers are at extending knowledge to students, how capable students are at explaining themselves and understanding teachers and one another, and

how effectively instructional discourse is organized to enable the exchange of knowledge.

My account thus far means that there are three sorts of social resources for the work of human improvement. One is the infrastructure of practice. In education that infrastructure includes curriculum, assessments, and teacher education, among other things. Infrastructure can be clear, with standards for work that are specified in considerable detail, or it can be ambiguous, with standards that are weakly specified or so jam-packed that key points vanish in the detail. It can be coherent, with standards for work that are linked to assessments and professional education, or incoherent, with weak or nonexistent links among the elements. The clearer and more coherent infrastructure is, the more likely it is that shared occupational knowledge can develop. Absent such infrastructure, it can be very difficult to build and accumulate common knowledge in any occupation. Workers can improvise, each creating his own version of the trade, but without some elements of coherent infrastructure, work can vary widely, and key elements must be reinvented every time someone begins.

Mutual commitment to improvement is a second sort of social resource. It is so fundamental that when clients and practitioners mobilize it themselves, despite other forbidding circumstances, they can do good work. Occasionally fine teaching in poor schools and occasionally helpful psychotherapy in state mental hospitals are examples. In such cases the social resources that are mobilized in what we think of as inside the work neutralize the negative effects of the social conditions that we think of as outside the work. Of course, mutual commitment to improvement is influenced by the attitudes that clients and practitioners bring to the work and by practitioners' efforts to engage them, but the organization of

work—the extent to which there is agreement about the results of practice, the extent to which responsibility for producing results is shared between clients and practitioners, and the extent to which the work flows from mutual choice—also influences mutual commitment to improvement.

The work that practitioners and clients create together is a third sort of social resource. In education that comprises resources that are devised and deployed in the three domains discussed earlier: knowledge extension, the organization of discourse, and teachers' acquaintance with students' knowledge.

The three sorts of social resources are interdependent. Absent mutual commitment to improvement, clients and practitioners can hardly begin work, let alone succeed, even if there are elements of infrastructure. Similarly, even with infrastructure and mutual commitment, the extent to which a practice of teaching can be cultivated depends on how well teachers and students create social resources in instruction with knowledge extension, instructional discourse, and acquaintance with students' knowledge.

I refer to these three factors as resources because they do not cause practice; only clients and practitioners do that. How resources enable or inhibit practice depends on how students and teachers use them as they extend and access knowledge, create discourse, and acquaint themselves with each other's knowledge. Teachers and students are neither pawns of social forces nor superheroes who overcome adverse conditions by trying harder and being more able; their work is the joint outcome of the resources they bring to the work and the social resources that they create in and through the work.

I discuss two of the three social resources sketched above in the rest of this chapter: infrastructure and mutual commitment. In

the three chapters that follow this one I discuss the social resources that teachers and learners fashion together in classrooms, and their interaction with the social resources discussed here.

Infrastructure

Skilled occupations cannot thrive without the extensive technical and professional affordances that enable work. Those include socially accepted views of the proper terrain of work; the sorts of problems that practitioners can claim to solve and the results that should be expected; the specialized knowledge and skills required to solve those problems; the specialized terminology needed to discuss, plan, perform, and assess work; the education that prepares people to work and to improve; norms and standards that inform judgments about the quality of work; the organized intelligence that influences the invention of new tools and technologies; and procedures to deal with unacceptable work. These things make up the socially organized infrastructure that undergirds skilled occupations. I term them "infrastructure" because they quite literally enable and sustain work.

In some occupations some infrastructure is contained in manuals that set out standards for materials and procedure. Electricians and plumbers have such reference works, and the *Physicians' Desk Reference* and other reference works, several now online, contain current medical knowledge of problems, diagnosis, and treatment. There also is continuing education of various sorts, and researchers, professional agencies, and regulators provide advice concerning standards of quality for drugs and procedures. Some other skilled occupations have fewer explicit standards or reference works. Top-quality cooks serve apprenticeships, and some attend schools

in which they learn the skills, norms, knowledge, and work habits of quality cooking, but there seem to be no common explicit standards.

Infrastructure is usually a creature of occupations. Plumbers and electricians play a large part in devising codes, sponsoring apprenticeships, and setting standards of work and material, and medical and legal organizations are influential in setting standards for practice, overseeing examinations for entry to the profession, and professional education. State governments sponsor these activities to one degree or another, but representatives of the occupation have a central role.

Teaching in U.S. schools is a different story. The infrastructure that is available to workers in other occupations is not available to teachers, and teachers do not play a central part in setting standards of occupational quality. Most developed nations have common curricula or curriculum frameworks, common examinations tied to the curricula, common educational practices that are grounded in the curriculum, teacher education that focuses on learning to teach the curricula that students will study, and a teaching force whose members succeeded with those curricula and exams as students. These social resources roughly parallel the elements of infrastructure that support other skilled occupations. By themselves these elements of infrastructure do nothing—much depends on their design and use. But if designed well they do create opportunities for use. Teachers who work with them can use them as a common framework to set academic tasks that are tied to curriculum and assessment, to help define common valid evidence of students' work, and to develop a common vocabulary with which to identify, investigate, discuss, and solve problems of teaching and learning. If these elements of infrastructure are well designed and appropriately used,

the elements of infrastructure can support quality work and reduce the need to invent or adapt resources that teachers would require to do such work on their own.

Teaching in the United States has an infrastructure of sorts, but it has few of the attributes sketched above. It is not mostly the creation of the occupation; unlike plumbing, law, or many other occupations, guidance for teaching has been created by agencies that lie outside the occupation. They include universities that educate teachers; state education agencies; text and test publishers that create materials that teachers use; state and local agencies that adopt texts and tests; state and federal policies that try to regulate the content and quality of teaching, define the outcomes of teaching, and set the conditions of teachers' work; and private agencies that interest themselves in the content of schooling, including evolution, religious belief, writing, homework, relations with parents, sex, health, nutrition, and much more. This list only begins to name the salient organizations and only hints at the blizzard of guidance and regulation that falls on teachers.

This weak infrastructure has little resemblance to that of other skilled occupations. There are many different and frequently divergent conceptions of quality instruction rather than one coherent conception. Some are evident in federal and state policies that now focus on students' test scores, while others appear in advice from professional organizations and parents' groups and advocate attention to literature, the arts, character, disabled children, academically gifted students, and several other matters. Conceptions of quality work differ, diverge, and often conflict. The result has been a hodgepodge of more or less urgent advice that arises from more sources than one can conveniently count. With a few exceptions, however, the guidance and regulation that might support any par-

ticular conception of quality practice are weakly developed and little elaborated, if at all. Those who offer advice are much more adept at announcing what should be done than at describing how it might be done, what it would take to do it well, and how we would know if it had been done well. With the exception of the National Board for Professional Teaching Standards (NBPTS), no organization of teachers has set standards of quality practice, devised means to discern whether they have been met, and used those means to regulate quality.

As a result, there has been no consistent conception of academic quality or progress, even within single subjects, and thus no guide to work for students and teachers. Although learning is believed to be cumulative, there has been common specification neither of the chief building blocks for learning any academic subject nor of how work on some building blocks would enable progress on more advanced blocks. There are competing conceptions of what learning is, what sort of building blocks there should be, and, often weakly specified descriptions of what is important to learn in each subject. In consequence, there has been no common, valid set of methods and procedures for instruction. Instead, a variety of methods and procedures exist, some passed down across generations of teachers who learn them from their teachers, others taught in teacher education, and others offered by advocacy groups of various sorts, including the partisans of "constructivism," traditional instruction, Montessori, gifted and talented instruction, "basic skills," and others. Most advice about instructional methods and procedures has unknown validity.

There are a few exceptions. Reading researchers identified teaching practices that are likely to benefit students in early reading; they could be part of an infrastructure for teaching, but the extent of their use in practice is unknown.[2] The Advanced Placement Program (AP)

in high schools is a subsystem of sorts with some elements of infra-structure, such as curricula and examinations tied to the curri-cula, and for several decades it was the nearest thing to a coherent infrastructure in U.S. education. But the AP lacks other elements of infrastructure, most prominently teacher education that is linked to curriculum and exams. In the 1990s NBPTS devised standards for teaching that were set by committees of teachers and subject-matter experts, and more than six thousand teachers have passed the Na-tional Board exams. That is impressive, but each NBPTS teacher works alone or with a few colleagues, so the standards are salient only to the National Board and have had little broad effect in or among schools. These exceptions aside, teachers have had no unified effort to set coherent standards, define essential practical knowledge, and set norms of quality.

Recent federal and state policies have tried in some respects to break this pattern. They set standards, but many have been over-loaded with detail. Most emphasis has been on tests, and there has been little attention to delineating quality in teaching. No Child Left Behind (NCLB) led to mostly weak standards and perfunctory attention to improving teaching. In the past few years, however, the Council of Chief State School Officers and the National Governors Association have launched the Common Core Initiative to write common standards for reading and mathematics for elementary and secondary schools. Unlike most previous efforts, the standards have been positively reviewed by knowledgeable commentators, and they could be used to help build coherent infrastructure. But even if the standards are well done, they are only one element in infra-structure, and the easiest to deal with. As one Common Core docu-ment noted, most of the work would remain after standards were set and adopted.

States know that standards alone cannot propel the systems change we need. The common core state standards will enable participating states to:

Articulate to parents, teachers, and the general public expectations for students;

Align textbooks, digital media, and curricula to the internationally benchmarked standards;

Ensure professional development for educators is based on identified need and best practices;

Develop and implement an assessment system to measure student performance against the common core state standards; and

Evaluate policy changes needed to help students and educators meet the common core state college and career readiness standards.[3]

These steps delegate nearly all the important work to states, but states and localities have rarely done such work, and their capability for it is modest at best. A recent study reported "Although most adopting states will require school districts to implement the common core state standards, the majority of these states are not requiring districts to make complementary changes in curriculum and teacher programs. Most of these states are expecting, rather than requiring, districts to undertake such activities as developing new curriculum materials and instructional practices, providing professional development to teachers and principals, and designing and implementing teacher induction programs and evaluations related to the standards."[4] This cautious approach will be reinforced by fiscal and political problems. As I write, early in 2011, many states are caught in serious fiscal shortfalls, and recent conservative victories

in national and state elections brought into office many Republicans who strongly favor local control. These developments are very likely to further impede implementation of the Common Core.

The Common Core is a promising beginning, but public education is still far from having a coherent and strong infrastructure. The commonalities that can be observed in many classrooms reflect the practices, habits, and knowledge that teachers learned as students from their teachers, not common standards, criteria of quality, and conceptions of instruction devised by discerning peers and leading professionals.

The sources of weak capability lie partly in the social and political organization of teaching, because public school teaching is a wholly owned subsidiary of state and local government. The conditions of teachers' work, their salaries, and standards of quality work are set by state and local governments, not by independent professional organizations. Some such organizations exist, but they have only weak advisory roles, so teachers have nothing like the influence on the conditions of their work that other skilled occupations have. At the same time, there are fifty state governments and more than fourteen thousand local educational authorities; each state and most localities set the conditions of teachers' work, their salaries, and any standards of quality. There is considerable variation in these matters within and among states, owing to the fragmentation of jurisdictions and large differences in their funds, educational resources, and human and social capital. Because federal and state efforts to create coherence are filtered through these fragmented jurisdictions with very different capabilities, implementation often has been incoherent.

The weak capability of education agencies also arises from Jeffersonian political ideas ("that government is best which governs

least") and the historically sketchy nature of state and local governments. State governments were weak throughout the nineteenth century and well into the twentieth, and their education agencies were especially weak. As late as the mid-1960s many state agencies had only a handful of professional employees, few of whom were aggressive managers. State governments outsourced the key elements of infrastructure: test and text publishing were left to private firms, and teacher education was delegated to higher education with little oversight. Conceptions of teaching quality were tied to teachers' years of education, their degrees, and their years of experience, none of which are closely related to the quality of classroom work.

These arrangements generate much advice about teaching and learning, but it is diverse and often divergent. Some of it contains resources that teachers can use if they have the will and opportunity, but it is far from coherent guidance for teaching, let alone ambitious teaching. Teachers who work with well-developed curricula, the means to collect timely evidence on students' work, and a repertoire of academic tasks that is referenced to curricula and assessments have less difficulty teaching ambitiously than teachers who must invent these resources. Those who aspire to high-quality work must, to an extent that would be remarkable in other skilled occupations, devise it themselves.

It would be fortunate if the Common Core did yield the intended infrastructure, but that will depend on how the elements of this infrastructure are designed and how well they are used, which in turn will depend on educators' capability and how society and government support the work. Standards alone will not do. For now and the near future, the lack of infrastructure poses large barriers to the cultivation of a practice of teaching because present circumstances leave individual teachers who wish to do ambitious work to

compensate for schools' and school systems' weakness. Individual teachers have done this, but the lack of a coherent instructional system to support them places an extraordinary burden on their knowledge, skills, and other personal resources.

Mutual Commitment to Improvement

Mutual commitment to improvement is strong in some situations but weak in others. Students and teachers in some inner-city Catholic elementary schools are intent on strong academic performance, but their colleagues in other inner-city elementary schools are not. Therapists and patients in some treatment settings work hard on the patients' problems, but there is little constructive work in other settings. I discuss two influences on such variation: social conventions about the results of practice and buy-in to work together.

Social Conventions about Results

Practitioners of human improvement strive for many different results. Psychotherapists attend to some sorts of learning, while teachers attend to others. Many teachers try to promote academic learning, but others focus on adjustment, vocational skills, self-concept, or ethnic culture. Traditional psychotherapists aim for insight and understanding, but behavior change therapy is becoming more common.

We take such differences for granted, as if they were given in nature, but they are only social conventions. Some are located in statutes, others in professional codes, and others in custom. Some have great generality, holding for an entire society or profession, while others hold for a community, a single practitioner and client,

or an organization. But however they are held and articulated, these are social creations, shaped by practitioners, clients, professional organizations, interest groups, and politicians. Conventions about the results of practice are not like shopping lists, quickly made up and easily altered; they are criteria for conduct and belief that we devise, apply, and change. They can be made with great deliberation or little thought. However they are made and unmade, they affect human improvement by shaping the problems that practitioners see, the solutions they entertain, and the resources needed to solve problems.

For example, teachers and students in Singapore or the U.S. Advanced Placement Program work amid social agreement about the results of their work, while students and teachers in high-school biology classes often work amid intense conflict about what students are to learn about evolution. Agreement can enable the creation or acceptance of elements of infrastructure, while conflict can impede it. How can one create acceptable criteria of quality practice or assessments of outcomes if there is intense disagreement about the results of work? Conflict about results also can impede mutual commitment to improvement. How can practitioners and clients commit to results about which they disagree? There also are appreciable differences in social conventions about who is responsible for results: Some teachers disclaim responsibility for students' learning, saying that their responsibility is to "put the information out there," while others assert that they have extensive responsibility for students' learning. If practitioners have most of the responsibility for results, they are more likely to have incentives to define results in ways that clients are likely to achieve. This can reduce conflict, but it also can impede demanding work because clients may feel unable to perform or may resist results with which they disagree.

Conflict and Consensus

Consensus about the results of practice can be a precious resource for clients and practitioners, but dispute about human improvement is widespread. Psychotherapy has been torn by competing schools of thought, and teaching in the United States has been the subject of arguments about purposes, methods, and criteria of success since state-sponsored schools began in Massachusetts. But for every case of conflict we can find another of consensus. The Republic of Korea, which is periodically shattered by bitter political conflict, displays little disagreement about the results of schooling. Singaporean schools present a similar picture. Japan has more conflict about schools, but it is tame compared with conflict about U.S. schools.[5]

One element of consensus in many nations is national examination systems. The exams are criteria of academic progress, of admission to further schooling, and qualification for work. Despite competition among students for academic rewards within many systems, there has been little dispute about the exams or their importance, and few alternative views of the ends of schooling or how to assess students' progress. In these cases schooling seems to rest on largely tacit agreement about the results for which students and teachers strive.

Matters have been quite different in the United States. Americans have a history of intense conflict over school outcomes and methods that dates back at least to eighteenth-century arguments between advocates of Calvinism and what became Unitarianism. Then and since, educators, public officials, parents, and community members have disagreed, often fiercely, about the appropriate results of school. Should children be taught to be patriotic and

God fearing, or should such matters be kept out of school? Should instruction focus on the written record of knowledge or on practical and usable knowledge? There also has been intense disagreement about how any given result might best be achieved. Should children be taught phonics and "math facts" by didactic and traditional means, or should they be taught to understand literature and mathematics by innovative means? Should African American students attend separate schools to save them from the ravages of racism, or do such schools perpetuate the problem they propose to solve? Americans also disagree about how results ought to be assessed: should a single set of tests be used to judge how well students and schools are doing, or should schools devise their own assessments of what they wish students to learn? Such conflicts boil up in classrooms, local communities, state governments, and the national legislature.

If assessment demonstrates agreement on the results of schooling in some nations, it is disputed in the United States. There has been little agreement about what tests should be used, or when, or for what purpose. There are many tests—students are tested more in the United States than anywhere else in the world—but the assessments are often inconsistent because there is considerable variation among them. Different tests of the same subject appear to assess different aspects of the subject. One of the few careful studies of agreement among tests focused on fourth-grade mathematics. Its authors observed, "Our findings challenge . . . [the] assumption . . . that standardized achievement tests may be used interchangeably."[6] Another source of inconsistency is decision making about the use of tests. Many decisions about testing remain local, but since 1994 states have made many more such decisions. A few districts use a single test for years, but others change tests every few years. School

systems also use one test at one grade and others at other grades, so there can be as many differences in assessment within districts as among them. Testing may have become even more varied in the past twenty years as policies that require testing have proliferated; more states use more tests, and localities devise or purchase additional tests.

Conflict about results can increase the uncertainty with which practitioners must cope. Teachers may see tests as a too-narrow version of learning, or they may worry about conflict among tests or inconsistency between tests and curricula, all of which have become more common as recent policies have pressed testing. In such cases and others, teachers must find ways to manage uncertainty about what to teach and how to use test results; they must cope with disagreement about the nature of their work as a condition of doing any work at all. Schools that are organized on the basis of mutual choice can set a standard for dealing with these issues at entry to practice, but compulsory public schools in the United States have tacitly delegated disagreement about the ends and means of education to teachers and students.[7]

Agreement about results can be a social resource. Teachers and students in Singapore and Japan are expected to teach and learn the mathematics in the examinations and related curricula; they still must make many decisions, but, unlike teachers in the United States, they cannot decide which version of mathematics they will teach and learn, or whether math is important enough to spend time on it. If teachers in such systems stray from the curriculum, students or parents may object. But if consensus may constrain uncertainty, it does not eliminate it. Math teachers in Singapore work within a specified curriculum, but they still confront many uncertainties: math problems can be ambiguous even if they are well

framed, and students often interpret a problem differently. The apparently simple effort to arrive at a common conception of a single math problem can generate appreciable uncertainty in a class. Teachers in France or Singapore face many uncertainties, even with social consensus about results.

In U.S. schools, these ordinary uncertainties of teaching and learning are amplified by social disagreement about results. Lacking consensus about the ends of mathematics instruction, some teachers teach the math that is measured on one or another standardized test. Others teach the math that is contained in one or more specialized tests, such as the National Merit Exam, the AP exams, or a state accountability test. Some others ignore tests and teach from the text that they chose, or that their school supplied. Some teach the math that they learned in a workshop, and many teach the math that they learned as students. Still others teach math very little. Often they teach some mix of those versions of mathematics. But whatever American teachers and students do, they must deal with issues that are not up for decision in other nations. The array of different views of results and the frequent lack of connection between curriculum and tests intensify uncertainty about what math is, what math might be taught, and how it might best be taught and learned.

In this situation, conflict and uncertainty about results more easily can become part of teachers' work with students.[8] If teachers must negotiate the results of instruction with students, doing so can enhance their dependence. Social consensus about the results of schooling eases teachers' dependence because teachers need not persuade most students to attend to exams and curricula if they seek academic success. American discord over the results of schooling intensifies a problem of practice that social agreement eases elsewhere.

Conflict or uncertainty about results also increases the risk and difficulty of ambitious teaching, while agreement about results reduces risk and difficulty. In systems in which national external exams are central, the risks of demanding work can be diffused as students and teachers work together against the exam, sharing risk; the aim is that everyone does as well as possible, and teachers position themselves as helpers of students working against the exams.[9] In contrast, if U.S. teachers propose demanding work, the risks can increase: students can point to others who are not doing such work, to parents or educators or public figures who question or oppose such work, or to classmates who did not do such work two years ago. Such conflict increases the difficulty of ambitious work, the likelihood of resistance, and uncertainty; it therefore can increase the appeal of a minimum program that most students can complete with relative ease. Teachers and students negotiate everywhere, of course, and educational purposes and methods must be reinvented as they are put to use. But teachers' dependence on students is more acute, and the risks and difficulty of their work grow, if they must manage conflict about results as part of their work.

The little consensus about results that exists in American education is found mainly in sheltered enclaves. Many independent schools rest on agreement about results; they educate for "character," for the AP examinations, for entrance to selective colleges and universities, or for some combination of these things. These aims are reflected in course offerings and tasks that teachers set. Some parochial and independent schools focus students' work on a limited range of subjects, in part to encourage common work.[10] Consensus about results also plays a key role in a few subsystems within public education, the best example being the AP. AP students and

teachers work together, preparing for external exams that are tied to course curricula. The exams are the same across schools and represent agreement about the aims of academic work that is quite unusual in the United States.[11] Teachers report that instruction is more satisfying in such enclaves, in part because work is less uncertain and risky.[12] But these enclaves have been relatively rare, and the islands of consensus contribute to the larger differences about the ends and means of education because each island defines distinctive aims, adding to the overall variety.

There have been several efforts to create consensus about results. In the late 1970s and early 1980s researchers and reformers promoted "effective schools," in which the formation of common goals was a central point.[13] Most advocates saw goal consensus as agreement on tests and often used the reform to promote rather limited instruction. They urged a managerial view of education and stressed the school head's role in establishing common goals for teachers and students. A few considered schools more broadly, either as complex organizations or as academic communities.[14]

"Systemic" or "standards-based" reform was a later and much more sweeping effort to create consensus about results. Beginning in the later 1980s advocates of this reform argued for more ambitious instruction. Schools would offer challenging work that was rooted in the academic disciplines, and students would become independent thinkers and enterprising problem solvers. Standards would create agreement about the content of instruction and would extend that agreement to the tests that were to be another element of instructional guidance.[15] Tests and standards would be "aligned" so that everyone would get the same messages about instruction.

Things turned out differently. There were few examinations and many tests. Despite state claims, few tests were keyed to a curriculum, in part because there were few curricula to which tests could be keyed. Once NCLB became law, given the generally weak capability of many schools and school systems, the tests often became a protocurriculum that created a consensus of sorts: many teachers tried to teach the basic, mostly quite low-level skills that the tests assessed. That was an improvement in many high-poverty schools in which there had been little effort even to do good work on basic skills, but it was not the consensus for which the advocates of systemic reform had argued. Instead of creating a social resource that supported more ambitious teaching, systemic reform often focused teaching and learning on low-level work.

At the same time, these reforms did help to create a policy framework and political climate that enabled some other promising endeavors. Several comprehensive school reform designs (CSRDs)—Success for All, Core Knowledge, and America's Choice chief among them—enlisted several thousand high-poverty public elementary schools. Each CSRD included curricula, teacher education, and designs for leadership and school organization that focused on student performance. These things, as well as opt-out provisions for teachers who disagreed, created more consensus than was common in U.S. schools. One result was the creation of systems of more coherent schools; another was better student performance. Several charter-school networks, including the Knowledge Is Power Program (KIPP), Achievement First, Aspire, and a few others, have created coherent small systems of high-poverty middle and elementary schools. These networks also have high levels of agreement on the results of schooling—improved student performance on state

and local tests is the chief result in question—intensive efforts to help teachers achieve the desired results, and systemwide coherence in instruction and support for instruction.

Consensus about results was an important part of what these CSRDs and charter networks did, but it was only part. These school systems also built infrastructure that included curriculum, teacher education, assessments, and leadership and organization. In addition, it is not obvious how to achieve the intended outcomes, even when they are scores on a test; the networks invested heavily and persistently in learning how to produce the outcomes. They instituted regular collaboration among teachers and school leaders to improve teaching and learning, and they monitored teaching and learning to discern whether the intended results were forthcoming.[16]

Agreement about the aims and content of instruction can be a significant social resource for instruction, especially for those who wish to do ambitious work, because it protects teachers from some of the uncertainty that accompanies such work, from the risk that uncertainty engenders, from disputes about the ends and means of instruction, and from students' resistance. If the Common Core is able to overcome the disputes that have punctuated schooling in the United States and retain its ambitious aims, if the states and their partners can build the requisite infrastructure, and if schools can put it into practice, it could become a framework within which agreement about the content and outcomes of school could grow. Moreover, the CSRDs and charter networks are useful examples of how to build systems of instruction that can turn such agreement on results into improved results; in the meantime, most teachers, students, and those who seek to improve instruction will have to cope with disputes about the ends and means of school.

Responsibility for Results

The responsibility for results varies among and within human improvement practices. Classical psychotherapy places much responsibility on the patient, a convention that is rooted in the view that because neurotics collude in their own problems, improvement requires that they take responsibility for solving those problems. If they succeed, they do so chiefly because they confront and understand their problems and find workable solutions. Therapists can help by asking salient questions, affirming insights, and offering support, but patients must recognize problems and work hard to solve them. Similarly, organization consultants often view poor communication, weak leadership, and ineffectiveness as self-inflicted wounds, the result of practices that organizations create and can change. Consultants can help diagnose problems and design solutions, but if clients do not take responsibility for the problems and their solutions, little will improve.

In contrast, schoolteachers have extensive and growing responsibility for results. State and federal policies have made teachers "accountable" for students' learning; state and local school systems have adopted testing programs that specify minimum levels of student performance, identify rates of success and failure for schools or school systems, and require schools to produce the stipulated learning. If they do not, teachers can be reassigned or removed, and schools can be "reconstituted" or closed. Students have no direct incentives to perform in such schemes, apart from whatever pressure their teachers can create. The assumption is that students' poor performance is due chiefly to teachers' weak effort, and that if teachers are made to take more responsibility for students' learning and work harder, students will do better. The re-

cent policies also owe something to the old American idea that learning is easy, and that students will learn if they are taught. Most educational theorists in the United States portrayed learning as natural and argued that any child can learn anything if it is properly taught. Jerome Bruner put it well when he wrote, in *The Process of Education,* "We begin with the hypothesis that any subject can be taught effectively in some intellectually honest form to any child at any stage of development."[17] The chief barriers to learning were said to be poorly designed curricula, inappropriate instruction, or indifferent teachers. I found no U.S. theorist who argued that learning is often risky and difficult, and no tradition of serious inquiry into risk or difficulty in learning, aside from special education.[18] Such ideas make it easy to believe that learning is chiefly the teacher's responsibility, and that students will learn if teachers do their jobs.

Public schoolteachers stand apart from other educators in this respect. Teachers in private schools can be assigned considerable responsibility for students' learning, though there is no formal accountability for students' test scores, but students also are held responsible for their learning. Students' responsibility eases the risk of making demanding assignments and reduces teachers' dependence. Professors in most colleges and universities are assigned no responsibility for the results of instruction; most treat learning as the students' business, and only a few institutions encourage professors to think and act otherwise. Few professors regularly check to see what students learn, apart from occasional exams that teaching assistants grade. Many design their classes to weed out all but those who learn well with little help; they aim not to improve most students' opportunities to learn but to assure that the fittest survive. Professors even assess instruction self-referentially; if they gave

a good lecture, they conclude that they taught well. Though there has been discussion of efforts to hold universities or professors accountable for students' learning, at the moment there is only talk.

Conventions about responsibility for results affect practice. Therapists, professors, and others are somewhat protected by the view that their clients bear heavy responsibility for the results of practice. If therapy goes poorly, the classical assumption is that it does so because of the client's neurotic resistance or some related problem. Therapists' risks in pressing for ambitious results also are eased, for classical psychotherapies assume that improvement is difficult and risky, and that many clients may not improve.[19]

My point here is not to defend conventions in higher education or classical psychotherapy, or to argue that it is unwise to assign teachers more responsibility for students' learning. My point is that responsibility for results, like other social resources of practice, does not operate in isolation. It would be constructive to urge teachers to take more responsibility for students' learning if other social resources of practice were present, including commensurate incentives for students to learn, consensus about the aims of practice, and arrangements for teachers to learn how to work more effectively. That is precisely what the charter networks and CSRDs discussed earlier do. But if those other resources are not present, as they have not been in most cases in recent public education reforms, simply assigning teachers more responsibility for students' performance is likely to yield perverse results. In response to recent state and federal policies, and absent substantial help in improving education, schools and school systems tried to protect themselves by lowering the test cutoffs for failure, simplifying content, or keeping weak students out of testing, in part because the efforts to increase teachers' responsibility for student learning did not offer

the other social resources of practice that would increase teachers' and students' chances of success.[20]

Human improvement is not like occupations in which objects or ideas are fashioned. A carpenter's specialized knowledge and skills are his distinctive resources; given decent materials and working conditions, he can create decent results. Holding carpenters responsible for results can make sense, other things being equal. But teachers need much more than their own knowledge and skills to do good work; they also require students' skills, knowledge, and commitment, as well as an environment that supports their work. These things are never under teachers' exclusive control and often are quite far outside it; because teachers' knowledge, skill, and commitment are only a few of the resources required for good results, increasing only their responsibility for results is likely to be counterproductive.

Buy-In to Work Together

Differences in the strength of mutual commitment to improvement also arise from the nature of practitioners' and clients' buy-in to work together. Buy-in is influenced partly by clients' and practitioners' attitudes, and partly by two social arrangements that bring them together. One of these arrangements concerns acceptance—the means by which practitioners or agencies decide which clients they will work with, and under what conditions. Some practitioners and agencies accept very selectively, admitting only people who are unusually able, needy, or intensely committed. Others are less selective; they may admit all who choose the service or who are eligible on the basis of age or other conditions, or the service may be compulsory. The other, complementary arrangement concerns

enrollment—the means by which clients find their way into work with practitioners, which influence the engagement with which clients enter.

Acceptance and enrollment count because they can mobilize or erode mutual commitment to improvement. If an agency or practitioner accepts very selectively, and if only able and eager clients enroll, clients' and practitioners' work together is likely to be constituted by the resources that flow from mutual choice and a sense of being special. Clients and practitioners not only select each other but also are set apart by their shared purpose and strong engagement, which can endow practitioners and clients with extraordinary social resources. But if agencies accept all who are eligible because of age, or if clients are compelled to enlist, practice is likely to be constituted by compulsion and a sense of the ordinary, because agencies and practitioners choose none of those who enroll, and many clients might not have enrolled if they had a choice. The work often is not defined by special aims or commitments, and practitioners and clients often must cope with social resources that inhibit ambitious work. In both cases the resources are not of practitioners' making, but in the former case those resources increase the chances that practice will prosper and desirable results will ensue, while in the latter the resources reduce those chances.

Acceptance

Clients are accepted for improvement in radically different ways. Table 4.1 displays several of the chief alternatives. In some cases practitioners or their agencies restrict acceptance to those who are specially qualified (first column). Private psychotherapists usually accept clients on the basis of commitment, ability, and interest, as do elite private schools, colleges, and universities and their gradu-

Table 4.1. Conditions of acceptance

Selective	Universal
Agencies and practitioners limit acceptance on some basis. Examples include admission to private schools, universities, and magnet schools, as well as to private psychotherapy, drug treatment programs, or programs for the disabled.	Agencies and practitioners put no limits on acceptance. One type is voluntary: improvement is offered to all, but at clients' choice. Examples include many community colleges and walk-in clinics. Another type is compulsory: improvement is required of all who are eligible. Examples include public elementary and high schools.

ate and professional schools. Some magnet schools, however, use only interest and commitment. Clients may be accepted on the basis of need, that is, because they have unusually grave problems, or ordinary problems but extraordinary constraints in solving them. Special schools for troubled youth may accept on the basis of need, as may some drug treatment programs and programs for disabled students. Selective acceptance can operate at any level of practice or at several levels at once. An entire practice or sector of practice may be selective, as in private psychotherapy; one sector of a selective practice may be very selective, as psychoanalysis was within psychiatry for many years. Teaching advanced graduate or professional students often is selective, even within relatively unselective universities, and it is superselective in some eminent universities.

In many other cases acceptance is universal, without special qualification (second column). One version of unselective acceptance is compelled for all, and clients have no choice about inclusion, whether they desire improvement or not: public schools are the chief U.S. case

of this sort, because school attendance is required for all children of a certain age. Another version of unselective acceptance is choice within universality, in which everyone is eligible but improvement is offered only to those who present themselves. For instance, many community colleges are open to all or nearly all who apply, irrespective of prior education.

Each form of acceptance is connected to a comparison, and the comparison is crucial because it helps to define the meaning of acceptance. If students with disabilities or learning problems are selected for special treatment on the basis of need, the comparison is "normal students" who require no remedial treatment. In this case the selection for special treatment also makes it difficult to avoid stigmatizing those who are treated. When students are selected for special treatment on the basis of their unusual ability, the comparison is to all students, many of whom are less able. In this case it is difficult to avoid stigma, or a sense of unfairness, for those who are untreated. More generally, one liability of U.S. public education is the comparison that it forecloses; because nearly everyone attends without qualification, it is unspecial, and this characteristic erodes perceptions of its quality. Compulsory and universal attendance interact with American attitudes toward education, to reduce the appeal of public schools. "Common" schooling once was a badge of distinction, in the early decades of elementary (and later secondary) school attendance. The schools were not yet universally enrolled, which lent common schools a certain cachet in the eyes of many Americans. But as their inclusiveness became greater and school problems mounted, the schools came to seem merely common.[21] Part of the appeal of private schools arises from the comparison that they offer to the large, gray public system; hence private schools often seem special, even when their edu-

cational quality is no better or even worse than that of some public schools.

Acceptance can occur in contrary ways within the same organization. A modest portion of a highly selective agency may be quite unselective, as in admission to classes within elite private high schools. Conversely, highly selective programs often subsist within entirely unselective agencies, for example, the Advanced Placement Program in public high schools, occasional schools for talented students among hundreds of neighborhood schools in a city, or a single class for able students in an otherwise ordinary school.

However it occurs, selective acceptance can create social resources of practice in several ways: the concentration of talent, the concentration of interest, the concentration and mobilization of commitment, the creation of mutual obligation, and the prospect of deselection.[22] These often overlap in practice but can be distinguished in analysis. The concentration of talent is the most familiar. The Advanced Placement Program skims promising candidates from a large and very mixed pool of U.S. high-school students; elite colleges, universities, and private schools draw the ablest applicants from large pools of remarkably talented candidates; the Harlem Street Academies drew the best applicants from larger pools of potential students. In these cases practitioners work with a small and special fraction of those who might be improved. The comparison for selection in these cases is the mass of potential clients who are presumed to be less talented or interested, and a smaller group of talented but rejected applicants. Unless unconventional indicia of talent are employed, only a few can be special.[23]

The concentration of interest can be more inclusive. City school systems have created magnet schools that cater to students' interests in mathematics, music, foreign languages, the arts, and

other educational specialties. Subject to the availability of places, schools admit students who can make a case for their interest in the school's program. If there were enough such schools and if all students had active academic interests, each student who wanted a particular type of school program might be chosen by a school that wanted that student.[24] In that case the comparison for selection would be the range of diverse interests in a population, not a dull and drab mass out of which an interested few were sorted. In such a hypothetical case most schools and students might be special.

Either sort of selection can be supplemented by the concentration and mobilization of commitment. Psychotherapists often look for patients who see that they have a problem, feel that they need help, can pay, and seem likely to stay the course. Selective schools and universities look for students who can make a convincing case that they know what the institution has to offer, deeply want it, and signal that they are likely to use it well. Clients' commitment also can be mobilized by invitation to join a select group: students who are accepted by Phillips Academy Andover, Harvard, or public schools of choice in Harlem may be galvanized to do better work because they have been chosen by such a special institution, and because they work with others like themselves whose acceptance marks them as special.[25] In such cases selection can enhance clients' performance by mobilizing their desire to do good work, which enhances their capacity to do such work. If so, can we distinguish the talents on which selective acceptance capitalizes from those that it enhances or creates?

Selective acceptance also works because it usually contains the prospect of deselection. If clients do poorly, they can be warned: improve or leave. Psychiatrists sometimes discontinue treatment with

patients who fail to engage their problems, and selective schools and universities sometimes dismiss students who do poorly or fail to play by the rules.[26] Knowledge of that prospect can mobilize commitment. But that leverage may be qualified by other considerations. Some are economic. Psychiatry has moved dramatically toward less selectivity as insurance companies increasingly refused to reimburse the cost of "talking therapies" in the last two decades. A recent report in the *New York Times* revealed that because insurance companies only reimburse for diagnosis and drugs, not classical talk, psychiatrists take many more patients and limit sessions to 15 or 20 minutes for brief interviews and drug prescriptions.[27]

Finally, selection can enable agencies and clients to cultivate a sense of mutual obligation. One can think of selection as an occasion for agencies or practitioners to make a promise to clients: "Improvement is likely if you maintain your commitment, but your failure to do so may be grounds for us to break the contract. Hence we expect you to do your best to succeed." Such statements are much more difficult to make when agencies promise to improve all comers. Those agencies tend to make a very different and unconditional promise: "Improvement for all here." That they assert the capacity to redeem all comers is not surprising, for without this claim, how could they justify accepting all clients? But having made this promise, how are they to keep it? One problem, already alluded to, is that deselection is more difficult in agencies that promise or compel improvement for all. To discharge clients is to imply that the promise—and thus the agency that made it—failed. If agencies assert that they can improve everyone, what can excuse a client's failure or termination? To promise universal improvement is to leave agencies and practitioners fewer grounds on which to qualify their obligations to clients. That can lead practitioners to reduce the improvements that

they try to make, as a way to create some success, and so reduce the prospect of a broken promise.

Something of this sort occurred in public education: universal acceptance and compulsion led to unqualified promises of improvement that understated students' part in their betterment and overstated schools' and teachers' efficacy. As public schools in the United States moved toward nearly universal attendance between the late nineteenth and mid-twentieth centuries they created student ability grouping systems, varied curricula, and social promotion, to make it much easier for students to "succeed" in school without succeeding educationally.[28] The more schools delivered on their promise of equality through universal enrollment, the more inequality they created in the education they offered. The response to that inequality, in the late twentieth and early twenty-first centuries, has been for governments to extend and intensify compulsion in public education with requirements for teacher and student performance, while also pressing for more choice, more diversification of schooling, and the creation of markets for schooling.

Enrollment

Acceptance is never enough. Clients' enrollment also is essential in the constitution of mutual commitment, for it is the enrollees who are to improve. Agencies or practitioners create conditions of enrollment as they design voluntary or compulsory schemes to accept clients, but clients' participation is never automatic. They reject improvement even in totalitarian societies, and rejection is much more common elsewhere. Americans regularly resist compulsory efforts to educate them or improve their mental health. Able math students often resist learning literature, and literature students regularly return the favor. Highly motivated psychotherapy

patients resist attention to particularly sensitive problems. Clients must enroll in their improvement even when they are chosen by practitioners or their agencies.

Table 4.2 displays the two chief alternative means of enrollment. Enlistment is at one extreme (the first row): one decides that one will undertake some program of improvement, actively searches out an agency or practitioner, and asks for assistance. If the person is accepted, he or she begins. The decision to enter private psychotherapy is one example; an organization's request that consultants diagnose its problems and prescribe solutions is another. Enlistment is the most typical form of enrollment in human improvement.[29] In addition to psychotherapy, it is commonly found in graduate and professional education, in private schools, and in some public schools of choice.

Assignment is at the other extreme. People are required to work with particular agencies or practitioners; if they wish to improve, they must accept the assignment. Clients are expected to comply,

Table 4.2.   Enrollment alternatives

Enlist	Students apply to private schools, selective universities, or particular teachers within schools. Prospective patients apply to private psychotherapists. Organizations seek help from consultants.
Be assigned	Clients are required to work with an agency or practitioner. Students are required to take a particular course. Patients are committed to mental hospitals.

either because law or some other authority requires it, or because improvement is asserted to be in their best interest or in the interest of their family, their firm, or society. If clients demur, they may be penalized. Schooling contains many examples of assignment. Students are assigned to public schools on the basis of age and residence and are assigned to teachers within schools. Students in private schools and universities often are assigned to required courses and teachers. Middle- and lower-level employees in firms often are assigned to work with consultants whom top executives hired to improve the organization. And some people wind up in psychotherapy because courts, civil procedure, employers, or family members require it.

There are many points between these extremes where enlistment and assignment mix. Some state mental hospitals allow patients to choose whether to enlist in psychotherapy after they have been committed. Public education offers many enlistment opportunities within compulsory attendance. For instance, although states require schooling, some permit families that desire home study to enlist in it; in this case, compulsory school is said to mean compulsory education. Students also enlist in nonpublic schools in all states, although the supply of such schools is often thin and the cost often is steep. Additionally, U.S. high schools offer students choices of their course of study and classes, and there are special programs for students with various needs or wants. Increased legal, economic, and social pressure to attend school has led to more choice about the sorts of schooling students might receive, and thus more opportunity for enlistment within compulsory education. One fascinating current feature of U.S. public education is the coexistence of increased compulsion and punishment

for nonperformance, on the one hand, with increased choice on the other. Though the two may seem mutually exclusive in logic, they are quite compatible, for more compulsion has created or amplified pressure for choice.

The dynamics of enrollment vary. In enlistment, improvement begins with a pledge of commitment: clients promise to play by the rules, to apply themselves, perhaps to pay, and to do their best. Such promises often are at issue in applications to schools and colleges, in interviews with admissions officers or therapists, and in discussions between executives and organizational consultants. Although the promises often are required for treatment, they offer opportunities for practitioners to reciprocate. In contrast, clients who are assigned need make no such pledge when they enroll. When patients or students are required to work with particular practitioners or agencies, they need not apply, perform in interviews, or participate in discussions as a condition of entrance or participation. They are offered no opportunity to pledge their commitment.

In fact, in such cases it is agencies or practitioners that explicitly or implicitly pledge to improve clients as part of their charter as compulsory agents. But there can be no improvement unless the conscripted client decides to enlist in it. That is a source of considerable worry for teachers in public schools in the United States, especially in secondary schools, as they try to "motivate" students (i.e., encourage them to enlist in learning) who seem indifferent. In such cases teachers are caught between the school system's promise to improve all comers, on the one hand, and the resistance that compulsion and the lack of choice often foster in students, on the other.

A related difficulty is that compulsory enrollment can lead to punishment for noncompliance and more compulsion. In U.S.

public schools these punishments were at first attached to truancy, but as schools recently have been pressed to deliver on their promises of improvement for all, enforcement has intensified. Truants have been threatened with cancellation of their driving licenses, and their families with loss of welfare benefits. The scope of enforcement and punishment has broadened from attendance to academic performance. All states and localities now require that students perform at specified levels because of federal and state laws, and some require that students pass exit exams. Compulsion also has hardened and is now associated with punishment for lacking improvement. But as compulsion becomes more rigid and enforcement more severe, improvement agencies have less and less room to qualify their promises in ways that could help create mutual obligation with clients. As the opportunities to mobilize clients' commitment are correspondingly reduced, so are many possibilities for improvement. Reciprocity is less of a problem when improvement is made available to all, but on a voluntary basis, for in such cases sponsors only persuade and induce. For example, political and corporate authorities encourage enrollment in community colleges, but they do so by making arguments about the value of further education and offering incentives in the form of low tuition, easy program design, and the like. Sponsors offer but do not require improvement and leave clients free to avoid it or to enter. By offering clients a way not to enroll, agencies and practitioners open room to qualify their promises to those clients: they will help anyone who makes a commitment to improve herself or himself.

Enrollment always has two sides. The arrangements for acceptance that practitioners and agencies devise influence clients' opportunities to enlist or to be assigned, but no improvement can occur unless clients enlist. Teachers who face classes full of as-

signed students often can make no progress until they persuade their charges to enlist in learning. Such persuasion is a continuing feature of teaching in U.S. public schools, where teachers often struggle with the combined effects of compulsory attendance and the low esteem in which many hold academic education. Despite that norm, students sometimes enlist in efforts to improve them, even when agencies offer no alternatives, seem indifferent, or discourage their efforts. Some university students enlist in learning despite the presence of thousands of classmates in huge compulsory lectures or numbing televised classes. Some high-school students enlist to learn in general-track classes to which they have been assigned, in which few students or teachers display much interest in instruction. Students sometimes enlist in learning in schools that have cynical teachers and indifferent or hostile students. Whether or not agencies offer opportunities for clients to enlist, people are not puppets; agencies or practitioners can contribute to the constitution of practice by the opportunities that they offer, but only clients can take or leave those opportunities. Whether and how they take them depends partly on what is offered, but clients always have choices about enlistment, if only the intensity of their engagement with their assignment.

Interactions

Acceptance and enrollment interact. Table 4.3 displays several of the chief combinations. Mutual choice, when practitioners or agencies selectively accept clients who enlist with them, is at one extreme (cell 1). Compelled improvement, when practitioners are required to work with clients who did not choose them and whom they did not choose, is at the other extreme (cell 4). The other alternatives are more mixed. In some cases clients enlist in universally

Table 4.3. Acceptance and enrollment

Conditions of enrollment	Conditions of acceptance	
	Selective	Universal
Enlist	(1) Mutual choice. Agencies and practitioners accept clients who wish to enlist. Examples include private-school or university enrollment and private psychotherapy.	(2) One-sided choice. Improvement is open to all, but clients must enlist. Examples include many community colleges, walk-in clinics, and upper secondary school in many nations.
Be assigned	(3) Mutual choice at the agency level, but clients are assigned within the agency. Examples include required courses in elite colleges and private schools and assignment of patients to therapists in private clinics.	(4) Compelled improvement without choice of agencies or practitioners. Examples include elementary-school attendance in the United States and required therapy in state mental hospitals.
Mixed	(5) Clients enlist in selective programs within compelled improvement. Examples include the Advanced Placement Program in U.S. high schools, voluntary psychotherapy in state mental hospitals, and school choice within compulsory education.	

available programs (cell 2); in others they are assigned within selective programs (cell 3); and in still others they enlist in compulsory improvement programs (cell 5).

Acceptance and enrollment affect practice by shaping the social resources on which practitioners and clients may draw. Consider mutual choice (cell 1). In such situations the difficulty of thought-

ful and demanding practice is eased by gathering able practitioners and clients who wish to work together. The concentration of talent and commitment eases the risks of difficult work, and practitioners can press for hard work with relative assurance that they will not be let down. That is partly because mutual choice limits practitioners' dependence on clients, since the terms of reference of work together typically include the understanding, sometimes explicit and sometimes not, that clients will work hard and do their best. Practitioners and clients persistently negotiate about their joint efforts, whatever the circumstances of their work, but mutual choice tends to frame those negotiations with a strong commitment to engagement on both sides. Although practitioners in these situations often wind up with able clients, unusual talent is not required; U.S. private schools are full of ordinary students who still work hard because that is part of the social contract.[30] In such circumstances, practitioners' dependence on clients is reduced by commitments that are set at entry and sustained by a school's culture.

Another reason that mutual choice can support ambitious work is that it constrains uncertainty by creating communities of practice. Such communities focus the aims of work and limit those to be improved to those who choose it. Catholic schools in America's inner cities accept a great variety of students, but they typically focus on rather traditional conceptions of academic achievement and accept students whose families agree to the schools' agenda. Hence teachers are less likely to have to cope with many students who are indifferent, dispute the teacher's approach to instruction, or prefer vocational studies or socializing with their peers.[31] Roughly the same thing can be said of admission to elite private schools, selective admission to graduate courses, and psychoanalysis; the social arrangements for acceptance and enrollment ease problems

of uncertain purpose and difficult work that often are acute elsewhere.

Mutual choice thus can mobilize powerful social resources of practice. It can present practitioners with clients who are likely allies, able and willing to do the work, and it presents clients with practitioners who are committed to their improvement. Mutual choice creates opportunities for clients and practitioners to generate and gather interest, commitment, and ability. It can help convince practitioners and clients that they are at work on special projects with special people, and that their prospects are good. To be chosen by those who may have the power to improve us, and who choose to work with us out of all those who might have been chosen, can mobilize hope and promise. To be chosen by enthusiastic and talented clients can similarly encourage practitioners. These social resources somewhat protect practitioners from some of the most painful predicaments of human improvement.

Mutual choice alone is not enough; clients and practitioners must additionally bend their knowledge, skills, and will to the work, for the existence of a social resource does not mean that it will be used, or used well. Advocates of charter schools have been dismayed to find that the mere existence of mutual choice does not assure improved education.[32] Some observers expect to find outstanding teaching in elite private schools and universities because entry is based on mutual choice, but much teaching in such places is ordinary or even dull and closely resembles teaching in much less selective schools. The content may be pitched at a higher level, and students may do better work, but the pedagogy is often pedestrian. The explanation is not difficult to find: teachers in such schools need not push far from ordinary work in order for their committed or talented students to do well. Extraordinary results

do not entail extraordinary demands on teachers. Because social resources can substitute for personal resources, practitioners may succeed without making heroic efforts.[33]

Many teachers in public schools do not have such social resources, because the schools are compulsory, and enrollment is universal (cell 4). Entry to practice is rarely organized around any expression of trust or strong mutual commitment to improvement. Such schools do not use enrollment and admission to mobilize social resources of practice: teachers work with many students who are not their allies in improvement, and many students have no teachers who want to work with them. Those conditions increase the risks that teachers take if they press for ambitious work. In contrast, teachers who choose to work with students who choose to work with them take fewer risks when they ask students to write a five-page essay on *The Ancient Mariner*. Equally able teachers in the two different sorts of schools face very different risks, owing to the different social resources of practice on which they can draw.

Compulsory improvement also can compound uncertainty. When clients' entry does not depend on mutual commitment to the means and ends of practice, teachers and students must settle those matters themselves. That can increase practitioners' dependence. If teachers propose to work in ways that require active engagement with demanding work, they often must persuade students to dig in, work hard, and sustain the effort, convincing and reconvincing students of the value of their work while trying to do it. Teaching in such circumstances can be the human improver's version of unrequited love: the prospect of success is appealing, but its costs can be enormous when students' and teachers' work is not framed by contracts to work hard together. The responsibility for improvement is one-sided.

The combination of compulsion and universal enrollment, absent organized means to mobilize and sustain mutual commitment, exposes teachers to the most difficult predicaments of their work. Schools make grand claims of improvement for all, but do not supplement teachers' responsibility to deliver on the promise with means to mobilize students' responsibility. The result is the assignment of great responsibility to teachers with few social resources to support their work. In contrast, schools that embrace mutual choice promise to improve those who enlist and can gain admission, if students and teachers pull their shares of the load. The Knowledge Is Power Program (KIPP) schools are a good example: like some other charter schools, students and families must promise at admission to work hard and do what the school requires. Those who do not or cannot, leave the program. Schools of this sort enroll more committed students, and they supplement teachers' responsibility with that of students'.

Mutual choice creates opportunities for applicants and practitioners to make contracts in which both agree to take a large part in the work; mutual choice does not require such contracts, but it enables them. Even with such contracts, practitioners and clients negotiate and renegotiate their commitments as work proceeds, but mutual choice frames these negotiations in a micropolitics of mutual responsibility. In contrast, agencies that enroll all comers without means to mobilize and sustain mutual commitment make grand promises while failing to mobilize the social resources that would help clients and practitioners deliver on them. The ideals that inform universal treatment in education have led schools to make sweeping claims for their power to improve everyone while removing a key element of human improvement. They create a micropolitics of agency omnicompetence, while at the same time di-

minishing clients' responsibility to take a major role in their own improvement. The ultimate expression of this unfortunate situation is recent state and federal policies that require schools to produce specific student outcomes and establish stiff penalties for teachers' failure to deliver but fail to attach any incentives or disincentives for students or families.

Public education in the United States is a paradox. It began in part as an effort to achieve greater equality and was informed by an appealing vision of the redeeming power of common school attendance. But those hopeful impulses helped to create a system in which many students and teachers can neither choose nor be chosen, and in which opportunities to mobilize mutual commitment to improvement have been eroded or entirely lost. The result has been an often-drab system in which few are treated specially, in part because all are treated.

Societal Influences

Although the social arrangements that I have been discussing are important, they are not controlling; other conditions can strengthen or weaken their effects. One such condition is beliefs about the value of formal schooling. Another is social pressures for academic performance. Still another is the demand from private firms and higher education for academic performance in elementary and secondary schools. All these conditions are stronger in some other nations than they are in the United States. The U.S. picture is not entirely gloomy, however; one encouraging development has been recent efforts to improve performance in otherwise weak schools by the recruitment of well-educated and engaged young teachers in Teach For America; another is the development of some charter

networks and some CSRDs that mobilize the beliefs and pressures that have often been weak in the larger system.

Social Beliefs and Pressure for Performance

Some societies hold intellectual work and academic accomplishment in high regard. Japanese and Chinese parents take education very seriously and hold teachers in high esteem. Japanese mothers encourage children's studies and work closely with them on assignments, and many work hard to create a home environment that is conducive to learning. Similar practices are found among Chinese parents. Japanese and Chinese mothers also seem to hold higher standards for their children and to have more realistic evaluations of their achievement than American mothers.[34]

In contrast, Americans have long been ambivalent about academic work, and anti-intellectualism is endemic. Americans tend to value experience over formal education and to value practical rather than intellectual content in formal education.[35] Relatively few mothers report close work with their children on academic tasks, or support for hard work and school success.[36] Students feel free to say that they attach little importance to book learning, and they hold their teachers in low esteem. Many teachers do not take education seriously. They often are poorly educated, do not pursue intellectual interests, have little regard for academic work, and focus more on "relating" to students or on extracurricular activities.[37]

Family life and culture thus support academic effort in nations like Taiwan and Japan but impede it in the United States. Cultural beliefs affect teachers, in part by affecting students' will to take on

difficult work. If American teachers press their students to do such work, they often swim against the tides of opinion in families, communities, and students.[38] That increases uncertainty and risk in instruction because teachers' demands conflict with students' experience and parents' expectations. It also increases teachers' dependence on students because their demands have little external support. If teachers succeed in ambitious work, they do so because they use their personal resources to make up for nonexistent social resources that would support demanding work. If Japanese teachers press students for serious work, they are likely to have parents' support, which limits teachers' dependence on students and reduces the risks of demanding assignments. If these teachers succeed, they do so partly because they can make use of abundant social resources of practice.

Employment and Higher Education

Postsecondary education and business also influence academic work by the incentives for performance that they offer. These sectors are the largest consumers of educated workers and signal the student attributes that they find desirable. Colleges and universities send mixed signals about the importance of strong academic performance in lower-level schools. Only a few highly selective colleges and universities have stiff admissions standards, while most have modest requirements. Students need only a thin record of academic accomplishment in high school, often only a C or low B average, to be admitted to many colleges and universities. Many other institutions require only high-school graduation, and many community colleges do not even require that. The positive aspect

of these standards is that they offer many students a second or third chance to make good, but they also signal that high-school students need not work hard in school to get into college or university, where many also will not work hard.[39] It can seem irrational for students who aspire to higher education to work very hard in high school unless they aim for selective schools.[40]

A similar situation has held for the employment practices of U.S. businesses. Few firms ask students for transcripts or teachers' references when they are considering them for employment. Even when firms do request transcripts, only a tiny fraction of schools supply them. The lack of employer interest deters students from thinking that grades, effort, or behavior count for jobs, and it deters teachers from thinking that their judgments about students can make a difference.[41] Hence it can seem irrational for students to do their best in school if they intend to leave high school for work. If they can get jobs without presenting evidence about their grades, school behavior, and teachers' evaluations, why should they work hard in school?

The lack of powerful incentives for academic work affect teachers and students because teachers depend on students' cooperation and engagement. If most students know that they need not push themselves in order to get jobs or get into college, it is difficult for teachers to press them to do their best. Teachers who do can run into problems if they ask students to do something that their friends down the hall or in the next school probably do not do. That increases the chances that students will complain, comply passively, or resist. To succeed in such circumstances, teachers must not only help students do the work but also continually persuade them that it is worth doing.

These patterns are unusual in some other nations. Universities in Japan and France, for example, lay great weight on students' high-school performance and on school exit or university entrance exams. If students wish to enter university, they must work hard in school and get good grades, prepare for exams, or both. Employers in many nations attend to students' secondary-school records when they are hiring. In some cases schools and employers work together to place students in apprenticeships or jobs. Teachers and students know that students who do not apply themselves and behave decently in school will have difficulty finding good jobs or apprenticeships. There are important rewards for academic effort and good behavior, whether students aspire to work or to further education. These systems have troublesome features, including early decisions about education or work and the effects for students who do not do well on exams. But there is little doubt about the importance of good academic work.[42]

Strong incentives for academic effort ease teachers' dependence on students, reduce the risk of urging demanding work, and increase the likelihood that such work will be done. When teachers or students press for outstanding performance, they can point to consequences beyond the classroom and can note that they ask for nothing different from what colleagues down the hall or in other schools are demanding; this argument can be a potent social resource for teachers and students. Students and teachers must apply themselves to do good work in any situation, but in some they need not struggle to persuade each other that the work is worth doing.

Although the likelihood of mutual commitment to improvement is increased by social support and incentives, it does not depend

only on these resources. I noted earlier that teachers' and students' actions within schools also create social resources, including mutual commitment to improvement. Well-supplied schools in advantaged communities can be dismal places that have little mutual engagement with academic work, and schools in disadvantaged communities, or classrooms in such schools, can be learning communities that are engaged and effective despite their surroundings. In Teach For America (TFA) these effects depend on the recruitment of unusually able college graduates, those who are most likely to bring intense commitment to the work, personal qualities likely to help them engage students, intense initial education for teaching, and continuing guidance and support as they teach. The TFA corps members' work ethic is intense during the school day and after, and their commitment to students is extraordinary. When TFA classrooms work, they exhibit unusual mutual commitment to learning. But the work is very difficult, most TFA corps members work alone or with one colleague in very difficult schools, their education for teaching is quite limited, and their schools do not necessarily use the corps members to help rebuild the schools and strengthen the faculty's engagement. One result is that corps members sometimes drop out during the first year. Despite these circumstances, the achievement test scores of students of TFA teachers are as good as or better than the scores of students of other teachers in their schools.[43]

If teachers who were as engaged and able as TFA volunteers worked in schools that were staffed with others like them, were organized to support their work with a culture of mutual commitment to learning, and had the wherewithal to improve their work, greater improvement would be likely. That is precisely what several charter networks do. The schools are public, but they are schools of

choice. Students and parents must commit to hard work, attendance, and the schools' rules in order to gain admission. The schools hire many former TFA corps members who also commit themselves to intense work, and they build organization within and among schools to improve teaching and learning. The results have been impressive; although the work is demanding and there is a steady turnover of staff, the schools create solid cultures of mutual commitment to improvement and infrastructure to turn that commitment into effective instruction.

The CSRDs that I discussed earlier have done similar things. They have a more difficult assignment because they work with established high-poverty public schools, they control neither teacher hiring nor student admission, and they must often cope with high mobility on both counts. But there is compelling evidence that they have strengthened mutual commitment to improvement, built infrastructure to improve teaching and learning, and improved student performance.[44]

Consensus about results and agreement about the importance of academic work are reinforced by societal pressures, beliefs, and habits in some nations. The combination is a significant social resource of practice because it limits uncertainty about instruction and eases the risks of demanding work. That resource has been weak in the United States, where conflict about results is reinforced by weak incentives for good academic work and ambivalence about academically demanding education. These factors have increased both the risks and difficulty of pressing students for demanding work, and teachers' incentives to settle for less. Despite the weakness of societal pressure and the damaging effects of deep poverty, though, some systems of schools have created the social resources

required to strengthen mutual commitment and improve teaching and learning.

The presence of certain social resources of practice can make it relatively easy to solve problems that seem difficult in some places, while their absence can make it relatively difficult to solve problems that appear easy in other places. One might say that the social resources of practice set limits on the problems that clients and practitioners must solve. All teachers negotiate with students to mobilize or maintain their commitment to learning, but those who work in schools and societies in which there are powerful incentives to work hard and do well, in which there is agreement about results, and in which there is an infrastructure that supports practice, deal with a relatively bounded problem. Their equally capable colleagues who work in schools and societies marked by weak incentives to work hard and do well, endemic conflict about the results of schooling, and little or no infrastructure face more pervasive and less bounded problems. In the first case teachers' problem solving has a relatively modest compass, while in the second it is broader. Teachers in both cases must solve continuing and important problems, but for some that work is eased by the presence of positive social resources of practice, while for others it is made more difficult by the absence of such resources.

Although such social resources are crucial, they do not operate in isolation. Teaching and learning are likely to prosper in the presence of such resources only if students and teachers have the wherewithal to use them well. If those conditions are met, teachers and students can do demanding work even in difficult circumstances. That is why strong incentives for educational results by themselves

do not create demanding teaching and learning. Such incentives can increase the chance that teachers and students will pay attention and work hard, they can reduce teachers' dependence on students when they press for ambitious assignments, and they can increase the chances that if innovative teaching and learning are called for, teachers and students will dig in and try. But strong incentives for results are of little use if teachers do not have the knowledge, skills, and courage to respond appropriately, and if other social resources are weak or absent. I take up these matters and their interaction with social resources in the next three chapters.

5

KNOWLEDGE AND TEACHING

Learning is an ordinary human endeavor. Anyone reading this page has learned many things, including how to dress, how to speak English, and perhaps how to drive a car or cook a meal. Some have learned more unusual things, like a foreign language or algebra. Presumably they have learned how to make sense of sentences like these. But if such learning is utterly commonplace, it also is quite remarkable because, almost by definition, it requires us to do things that we do not know how to do. I could not have learned to swim unless I got into the water and tried to swim, even though I did not know how. Unless I tried and failed, I could not begin to swim or hope to grasp what remained to be learned. But I could not swim. There was no help for it. I had to get into the water and thrash, choke, sink, wish I were somewhere else, and intermittently rue the day I decided to learn to swim. There was no other way to learn.

Learning is paradoxical. We can learn only by sailing the boats that we are trying to build. If we are beginners or even novices we cannot sail them very well, because they are not yet built, but we can build them only by trying to sail them. This is sometimes a delight, sometimes a puzzle, and sometimes a worry. Many readers

will recall the blank they drew when they first tried to swim, drive, or work an addition problem. Some will remember the ensuing delight and others the worry. But humans all over the earth learn millions of times every day.

Teachers face a different problem. They sail more finished boats and have at least a few ways to maneuver them. But their assignment is to reach out from craft already built and cruising a familiar course to learners whose boats are only begun and who are moving tentatively, are on a puzzling course, or are dead in the water. They do so in part by extending knowledge. They lecture, write, assign reading, compose computer courses, and in many other ways launch knowledge toward learners. Teachers' learning is an essential asset in such work because the more they know, the greater their resources for helping learners. But equally learned teachers extend knowledge in very different ways. Some treat it as the result of a practice of inquiry and try to make that practice accessible: they use metaphors, analogies, set problems, draw pictures and diagrams, and use other intellectual tools, all intended to make knowledge available to learners. They do these things in the course of setting academic tasks that are designed to enable learners to become novice practitioners of mathematics or history and thereby make knowledge their own. In these ways and others they turn their academic knowledge into social resources for instruction. Teachers who work in this way cultivate elements of a practice of teaching as they extend knowledge in ways that are calculated to advance learners' understanding.

Many other teachers present knowledge in finished form. Some math teachers work complex problems at the board, demonstrating polished solutions or proofs in an effort to represent the best work; then they tell students to "practice." Finished knowledge is an es-

sential asset in teachers' work because it is the sort of performance that learners should finally achieve; it nicely represents intellectual accomplishment in a field, and the more accomplished teachers are, the more finished their knowledge is. But extending knowledge in a polished and highly compressed form can be a liability because those formulations usually are quite remote from most learners' tentative efforts. Teachers who work in this way are often less effective at turning knowledge of academic subjects into social resources for instruction—that is, academic tasks and other instruments that enable learners to become novice practitioners of mathematics or history. They are less able to cultivate a practice of teaching because their approach limits students' access to knowledge.

Consider another metaphor. Teachers and learners face the same gulfs of ignorance, but from different sides. Learners must somehow build bridges across the gulf, but these bridges are often fragile because the learners work from relative ignorance. The teacher's assignment is to help learners build those bridges, but they work from greater knowledge. That they do so reflects a key qualification, for ignorant teachers would be no help. But their knowledge often leads them to see learners' work as fragile and jerry-built; they often respond by reminding learners of the finished formulation. Rather than helping learners construct and reconstruct bridges of their own, teachers present the finished result of their learning.[1] That reduces the likelihood that teachers can cultivate a practice of teaching, for it can limit learners' understanding.

That teachers do such things is no surprise, for to learn well is to consolidate knowledge, and once that is done, earlier formulations can seem clumsy. Finished work is much more elegant and pleasing, and it seems only right to convey it to learners because that is where they should wind up. The achievement of some intellectual

competence is both a necessary condition of and a limit on quality in teaching.

Knowledge Extension

Teachers commonly extend knowledge in finished form. One familiar example can be found in mathematics. Teachers from first grade to graduate school work problems as efficiently as they can. They stand at the board or overhead projector and announce that they are "showing" students how mathematics is done. Once the example is complete, students are enjoined to "practice," that is, to work the problem and others like it as the teacher did. These demonstrations present a condensed version of mathematical problem solving on the assumption that if students follow the example, they will learn. This sort of teaching in elementary classrooms often consists of a mechanized version of arithmetic, but in universities it often offers elegant examples of finished work. In either case teachers present instances of the desired end state of learning that are quite remote from the fits-and-starts ways in which mathematicians and students of mathematics actually work. Instruction in writing has been similar: teachers read good writing aloud, assign it to learners, or copy it on the board, then hand out paper and invite students to write a story or essay on a similar theme. The teachers appear to assume that in order to write well, one need only follow the example and practice, neglecting to mention that what they read often was the result of many false starts and revisions.

It has long been fashionable to scoff at such teaching; John Dewey was only the most distinguished of many commentators to deride it. Like Johann Heinrich Pestalozzi and others in Europe and the United States during the nineteenth century, he asserted

that presenting knowledge in its finished, "adult" form was a foolish effort to cram dead stuff into live minds. Dewey and others argued that knowledge should be presented so that it fitted with children's more concrete and vital modes of thought.[2] Jean Piaget gave these ideas scientific cachet in his studies of children's cognitive development. The idea that knowledge should be represented so as to accord with learners' stages of cognitive development became a sort of orthodoxy, especially in the emphasis on "concrete operations" in primary education.

These ideas captured an important intuition about teaching, but if it is foolish to extend finished performances to students, the foolishness is nearly ubiquitous. To grasp what it takes to construct a practice of teaching, it is helpful to understand why this foolishness makes such good sense to so many people.

Consider how we learn to use the clutch when we are beginning to drive. Teaching in this case often consists of the instructor saying something like "Just let the clutch out slowly while accelerating gently." Although this statement correctly describes the operation, it is a vastly compressed synopsis of an entire set of procedures. There is no reference to the many subroutines that contribute to successfully letting the clutch out slowly while accelerating gently. The teacher has extended a fair summary of what the intending driver needs to do, but like all synoptic teaching, it offers little sense of what is entailed in the doing. One reason that teachers find such synopses reasonable is that they seem transparently clear; experienced drivers have so thoroughly routinized and integrated the many subroutines contained in clutch and accelerator coordination that the synopsis accurately portrays their polished performance. The knowledge that teachers extend toward students in such cases is what they are aware of doing, so it is not surprising that they grow

impatient when students repeatedly stall the car or profess incomprehension. Nor is it surprising that such teachers respond by reasserting that "it's perfectly clear; just let the clutch out slowly while accelerating gently."

It is easy to say that teachers should explain or demonstrate, but their exasperated repetition masks a difficulty. Accomplished drivers would have to work hard to rediscover all the subroutines in their smooth clutch and accelerator work just to make them explicit to themselves and then turn them into a curriculum for learning to use the clutch. "Rediscover" is the appropriate term because learning to drive is in part a matter of learning and automating many operations, dispatching them from attention to leave the mind free to attend to oncoming cars or to passing a truck. But it is just those individual subroutines and their coordination that each new driver must learn, and to them, the teacher's compressed sentences are mysterious. That is not surprising either, because novices know nothing of the operations thus summarized and can barely perform as drivers—hence their baffled pleas to "please explain it just once more." Between teachers' impatiently repeated synopses and learners' pleas for more explanation lies a gulf that separates teachers and learners of many different sorts.[3]

Novices nonetheless do learn in the neighborhood of such teaching. They commonly put the hapless automobiles into a series of convulsive, choking fits and starts. Teachers grit their teeth or shout, "Floor the clutch," "Use less gas," or "Stop!" The wear and tear on cars and people can be appreciable, but most novices figure out a way to release the clutch while increasing the gas in trials and errors with clutch, gas, and auto convulsions.

There are alternatives. A teacher can begin by telling her student that the clutch permits drivers to make or break the connection

between the engine and the driving wheels, which allows drivers to start, stop, and change gears without stalling or stripping the gears. The teacher can then pull out a drawing of the drive train, locate the clutch in it, and display a working model of the clutch and trace its operation. She identifies the two plates that are the heart of the device, shows how they engage and disengage by being slipped together or pulled apart, explains that this frictional arrangement permits gradual engagement and disengagement rather than simple on/off action, and shows how slippage helps when starting and shifting through the gears. She tells the student to work the model and ask questions about it until the student seems to grasp the matter.

The teacher then does a dry run. She puts the emergency brake on, shifts to neutral, starts the engine, shifts into first, and slowly engages the clutch. When it begins to catch, she quickly depresses it to prevent a stall. She invites the student to repeat the steps verbally and trace the account on the working model. She then asks the student to slide into the driver's seat and practice the operations several times with the engine off. She follows his operations on the model and relates them to the model's movements.

When the student seems to grasp these operations, she asks him to try it with the engine on and the transmission in neutral. If that goes well, she asks him to release the clutch slowly and only partly with the engine on but the emergency brake engaged to get the feel of the clutch as it begins to engage. Then she drives to an empty lot, stops, and asks the student to start the engine, shift into first gear, and practice starting and stopping the car. Once that procedure seems to be under control, the teacher can begin to teach the student to shift through the gears while driving in the lot and then on a quiet street.

This unpacked approach offers novices opportunities to learn how to perform the operations involved in letting the clutch out slowly while accelerating gently. It does so as the teacher turns her knowledge and know-how into social resources of instruction: tools that learners can use, tasks that unpack the subroutines, and opportunities to practice in feasible portions. These social resources enable learners to become novice practitioners rather than purely trial-and-error learners. Of course, trial and error remain essential for learning because there is not enough time or energy to unpack everything, and learners sometimes venture into territory that their teachers do not know.

The approach in this example was not impossibly difficult to devise. Why, then, is synoptic teaching so common? It is not, as critics have said, foolish adherence to a bad habit. Synoptic teaching is deeply rooted in the ways in which we learn and hold knowledge. Consider another example. If someone asks us to "show me how you learned to swim," we typically demonstrate the result rather than rehearsing the learning. We get into the pool and swim as well as we can. If the questioner is learning to swim, we try especially hard to swim well in order to demonstrate how it is done. We can observe this aquatic equivalent of teachers' mathematical problem solving in swimming pools all over the land: what is important to the accomplished performer is the finished performance, not how it was learned. Intuitively, we teach by producing such performances.

It is not lack of alternatives that makes us do this. In principle one could first flounder, choke, thrash one's arms and legs, and sink. Then one could swim a few strokes clumsily and stop, gasping, and then swim a lap badly, and stand panting at the end of the pool. After a pause one could swim a few laps a little better, and so

on. If one proceeded in this fashion, one could indeed show the questioner "how you learned to swim." If the questioner sought to learn, the demonstration might have some pedagogical value, if for no other reason than that it would offer a sense of the trajectory of learning.

One reason that such demonstrations are uncommon is that we generally teach as we were taught. Although learning often progresses in fits and starts, teachers ordinarily see the fits and starts as mistakes that must be stamped out, or as "misconceptions" to be corrected. They rarely extend knowledge to learners in ways that capitalize on the learners' experiments, mistakes, and innovative ideas. Few teachers know how to unpack knowledge, partly because few were taught to do so in school, university, or professional study. When learners later turn to teaching, only rarely can they draw on experience that might help them unpack knowledge.

A less obvious but more important reason is that it becomes more difficult to re-create or appreciate novice performance as one grows more accomplished. Few good swimmers could spontaneously reproduce earlier incompetence, paddling as though incapable of swimming and then re-creating their progress to polished performance. To learn to swim well is to unlearn the bad habits, poor attitudes, and awkwardness of beginners and poor swimmers. Such unlearning is a crucial part of learning; one cannot learn to swim well without massive unlearning, and that is not unique to swimming. The more polished our performances become in any realm, the less we remember how we did things less capably. Novice performance is sometimes ingenious but frequently inefficient or clumsy. If we did not forget novice practices and ideas as we learned, every new performance would be a struggle to learn everything all over again. Psychologists, among others, commonly think about learning

as a process of adding something, but what is subtracted is no less important. If we did not forget much of novice performance, life and learning would be endless repetitions. Little would ever be solidly achieved because little would be forgotten. We would all be Sisyphus all the time.[4]

But if such forgetting advances learning, it can inhibit teaching. Like everyone else, most teachers have forgotten many experiences that might help them build bridges to learners. Like everyone else, they are encouraged to forget in part by the allure of polished performance. To be knowledgeable and skillful is to produce such work; the greater one's mastery, the more efficient one's performance. Mastery is something to be cherished no less in smooth driving over a winding road than in writing a historical essay or solving a physics problem. One reason that math teachers work problems as cleanly as they can is that elegance is a mark of good work; stumbling through problems piecemeal seems clumsy, even though that is what mathematicians usually do on the way to cracking them. English teachers read from Twain's or Hemingway's best stories rather than some messy early draft because it is lovely prose, the genuine article, the elegant writing that teachers hope students will produce and appreciate. What could be better than to launch such examples toward learners?

Another reason that teachers find it difficult to extend knowledge in unpacked form, then, is that polished performance is an expression of fine achievement and an essential means of communication among accomplished performers. Synoptic teaching often embodies crucial elements of the high culture and aspirations of a practice, be it physics or playing the violin. Finished knowledge also is utterly essential for good teaching. If teachers did not know what polished work was like, they could hardly know what they

wanted to achieve or offer examples of where learning should head. Without the knowledge and skill that such performances embody, teachers could not recognize signs of competent performance, inventiveness, insight, or misunderstanding.[5] However, polished performance also can impede the cultivation of a practice of teaching because its allure can keep teachers from opening knowledge to learners by enabling novice work.

Finally, unpacking knowledge so that novices can learn authentic practice is relatively rare because it is time consuming, messy, and demanding for teachers. As teachers offer students routes into knowledge by way of authentic performance, they increase the complexity of instruction. They enrich teaching and learning while they increase uncertainty; instruction becomes more difficult because the demands on teachers' knowledge, skills, and attention grow. If, in contrast, teachers extend knowledge in compressed form, especially in the school version of academic subjects, they reduce the complexity of knowledge and of extending it, they constrain the uncertainties of instruction, and they limit the attentiveness required to teach.

Given this discussion, it seems fair to say that it is an unnatural act to extend knowledge in unpacked form, in ways that enable learners to learn how to cultivate intellectual inquiry. This does not mean that such teaching is impossible. It is possible—after all, much of our civilization is composed of such acts. But teaching in this way runs contrary to so many deeply ingrained features of learning and teaching, that learning unfamiliar practices and unlearning familiar practices are required for teachers to perform in this fashion.

Knowledge

Although teachers extend knowledge in different ways, the knowledge they extend is not neutral. To be taught and learned it must be construed somehow, and it can be construed very differently. Some treat it as a body of established facts and procedures, while others treat it as developing, contested, and constructed. Many teachers and students of history act as though historical knowledge is an objective record of what happened, a view that has been familiar to historians and philosophers of history. The tracks of the past are out there, waiting to be dug up, dusted off, and recorded. Writing history is an objective reconstruction, and historians do it with a minimum of distortion; the better their work, the more closely they approach truth. But in another line of practice, knowledge of the past is inseparable from interpretation. Historians weave knowledge from their interpretations of artifacts and documents, their inferences from what contemporaries thought happened (which usually are woven out of what others thought and said), and their analyses of other observers' accounts. Knowledge is not out there to be found but is created as the mind makes sense of ambiguous experience. Historians construct accounts of the past that are plausible, elegant, or useful; they are truths of a sort, but they are partial, contested, and subject to change. Where some see discovery, others see interpretation.[6] These differences shape the knowledge that teachers extend toward learners.

The composition of the knowledge that teachers extend also differs. Knowledge in most fields comprises several elements: distinctive methods of inquiry and operations, special terminology, approaches to problem setting, and means to defend results. Special methods of historical inquiry include archival techniques, and in

literary criticism methods of textual analysis. Special terminology in mathematics includes signs, symbols, and terms like "addition" and "factoring." In literature it includes such terms as "character," "plot," and "meter." The specialized language of physics includes "mass," "acceleration," and "electron." From this perspective, to teach literature is to define or describe plots, or both. To teach arithmetic is to define the meaning of "+," to present examples of what it entails, or to compare it with such other terms as "−."

Problem setting entails defining questions in ways that can be productively handled within a field. In classical mechanics, physicists set problems with a special sort of abstraction: from many attributes of bodies in motion, they construct a few that permit calculation of acceleration, force, and mass. Hence teaching this subfield of physics might involve illustrating how problems are set up or presenting alternative but unproductive ways of setting them up. Historians also set problems, and teaching history might include demonstrations of how to work with archival sources to set up problems for research, analyses of other scholars' well- and weakly framed research problems, or both.

The defense of what one thinks one might know is also an element of most fields. Each field contains an array of means by which inquirers can check their own doubt about a result or respond to the challenge: prove it! Suppose, for instance, that a student doubts her solution to a multiplication problem and asks her teacher if it is correct. Teaching arithmetic in this case may include showing the student how to "prove" her answer—divide the product by one of the numbers multiplied and see if the quotient is identical to the other number multiplied. Or the teacher may tell the student to check the answer against the list at the end of the chapter. Similarly, many teachers show their students how to defend historical

knowledge by reference to established authorities—by checking facts and conclusions against reference works or texts—while others give examples of how to assess consistency between evidence and argument or consistency within evidence and within arguments.

To know any field implies that one knows something of all four elements: I could not plausibly claim to know arithmetic if I knew the signs and symbols but could perform none of the operations they entail, could not set or at least recognize arithmetic problems, and could not somehow defend my answers. But although all these elements play some part in knowing a field, teachers assign them different roles and weights. Some give pride of place to terminology and methods of inquiry, while others focus on the defense of results. Some focus on only one or two elements, while others try to integrate all four. These variations add up to different views of what it means to know a field, and thus to different versions of the knowledge that teachers extend to learners.

As I noted in Chapter 4, teachers' actions are influenced by the available social resources. In the discussion that follows, I consider knowledge extension chiefly in the social organization of instruction that has been conventional in the United States. That organization includes the absence of a coherent educational infrastructure and the lack of much common knowledge of teaching. At the end of this chapter I contrast knowledge extension in this kind of organization with knowledge extension in organizations that build a coherent infrastructure and common knowledge of teaching.

Many elementary-school teachers regularly give the lion's share of mathematics instruction to special terminology and distinctive methods and operations. They focus on identifying and practicing the operations for which the plus sign calls. They give little or no attention to the defense of results, and instead of attending to

problem setting, they accept problems as they are given in texts and worksheets. In contrast, some teachers devote much attention to setting problems and defending one's work. They present stories or puzzles that have quantitative elements, encourage students to transform them into mathematical problems, and discuss whether solutions make mathematical sense. Special terminology and methods play a role in these teachers' approach, but they are embedded in problem setting and defense of results.

Knowledge composition differs depending on which element has featured billing, and on how many elements are included. Our appreciation of how varied the knowledge that teachers extend can be is enhanced if we consider how compositional differences interact with differences in how teachers construe knowledge. Many math teachers attend to the defense of results as well as distinctive terminology and special methods, but they do so procedurally; proof is treated as a matter of checking with authority. They tell students to compare their answers with the sheet posted in the hall or the list at the end of the chapter. If there is a dispute, they refer students to the text, the answer sheet, or other books on mathematics. But a few math teachers treat the defense of results as a key part of making mathematical sense; they present problems that may challenge students' efforts to defend their answers and help students learn to justify their answers in ways that make mathematical sense. They cultivate students' capacity to make persuasive mathematical arguments, and they treat the difference between mathematically defensible and indefensible justifications as no less important than methods and results. As they proceed in this way, teachers deploy social resources that offer novices opportunities to become novice practitioners of mathematics.

Such differences bear on teachers' capacity to cultivate a practice of teaching. If math teachers drill students on the performance of

procedures, they need not cultivate a very complex practice, because the mathematical knowledge they extend includes little problem setting, proof, or justification of results. If they treat proof as a matter of checking with authority, they constrain complexity and limit their attention to learners' work. They do convey knowledge that mathematicians created, but it is what Dewey termed "inert," the result of inquiry divorced from the practice in which it was produced, criticized, and revised. Teachers who extend such knowledge need not think deeply about the mathematics or how they design it for learners. In contrast, when teachers frame lessons that invite students to discern the mathematical elements in a story or to develop mathematical justifications for their work, they increase the complexity of the knowledge that they extend, the attention required to teach, and the opportunities for students to become novice mathematical practitioners. This approach requires a more complex practice of teaching and places greater demands on teachers' knowledge, skills, and courage.

These differences affect the ways in which teachers manage their work. When the defense of results is treated mechanically, teachers and students need only check their work against some knowledge already given. That approach limits uncertainty and eases the difficulty of teaching and learning. But when the defense of results is treated as a matter of making good arguments, teachers and students reconstruct knowledge as part of their work together. That approach multiplies uncertainty and increases difficulty.

Interactions

As I compose this chapter, I can distinguish how teachers hold knowledge from how they extend it, but the two twine together as I teach. Professors who say that learners make their own sense of

things often present the material synoptically, as though they could construct knowledge for students. Other teachers who hold knowledge as though it were fixed unpack it somewhat for students. One must take account of such seeming inconsistencies to understand the role that knowledge plays in teaching, and how teachers manage the demands of their work.

Table 5.1 displays a few ways in which teachers combine views of knowledge with means to extend it; the four alternatives are far from the only ones, but they are relatively clear. In the most familiar approach, teachers hold knowledge as fixed and extend it in synoptic form (cell 1).[7] Most elementary-school teachers treat mathematics

Table 5.1.   Interaction between views of knowledge and modes of knowledge extension

Modes of extension	Views of knowledge	
	Fixed	Authentic intellectual practice
Synoptic	(1) Teachers extend facts and procedures in compressed form. They use few examples, representations, and the like.	(2) Teachers extend knowledge as the fruit of inquiry in compressed form. They use few examples, representations, and the like.
Unpacked	(3) Teachers extend facts and procedures in expanded form. They use examples, illustrations, and the like.	(4) Teachers extend knowledge as the fruit of inquiry in expanded form. They use many representations, illustrations, and the like.

Note: The alternatives sketched in this table do not take account of other important influences, such as how discourse is organized (see Chapter 6), and thus they do not exhaust approaches to teaching.

as an edifice of terms, facts, and procedures and extend it to students in finished packets of rules and numerical procedures. A teacher might present two-digit multiplication by standing at the board and beginning with a problem like 12×12: "The first step is to multiply 12×2, then write the partial product 24. Then multiply 1×12 (if you don't know these things, review your times tables), and write that partial product. Be sure to notice that this product is indented one space from the right; that's where lots of people go wrong. Then add the two partial products to get the answer."

In this case multiplication is extended in a few compressed gulps: problem recognition, times tables, rules about lining up partial products, and, with larger numbers, rules about carrying. Such work is familiar in universities; the mathematics is more advanced, but it often is presented as finished rules and procedures. Math teaching of this sort can be framed in drab workbook problems or quick and lively presentations, but both are synoptic. Many history teachers launch compressed narratives at learners; to learn history is to remember such narratives, and to teach history is to extend them. Although history of this sort often is one-dimensional, it can be delivered in lively tones with catchy examples. But that does not change the view of historical knowledge.

At the other extreme are teachers who offer access to knowledge as the output of intellectual inquiry, and who extend it to learners by creating opportunities for them to learn how to conduct such inquiry (cell 4). In teaching two-digit multiplication they try to make the conceptual structure of the operations apparent. They represent the numerical operations by drawing twelve groups of twelve dots each on the board, giving students dried beans to represent problems like 12×12, or asking students to fashion their representations of the operation and inviting students to explain

and defend them. They extend knowledge in a variety of forms: they present examples, make analogies, use metaphors, invent alternative depictions, and the like. Each representation offers different materials with which to make sense of multiplication and different opportunities to traverse the terrain from somewhat different perspectives. Most important, teachers embed these representations in opportunities for students to do the mathematics, to frame and solve problems, and to explain and defend their work—in a word, to work as novice mathematicians.

History differs from mathematics, but there are similarities in how teachers of this sort present material. In teaching the Holocaust, they may use excerpts from prisoners' journals, news stories of the period, documents in which the Final Solution was set on its way, propaganda films, and interviews with Nazi officials. In such teaching the past speaks in different and sometimes opposed voices, and teachers use them to challenge students to do history—that is, to make sense of the evidence and offer a defensible interpretation of it. Teachers set assignments that ask students to conduct historical inquiry.

Teaching of this sort opens many opportunities to connect teaching and learning, but it makes formidable demands on knowledge, skills, and other resources. Teachers have to be accomplished students of history because they cannot compose such materials unless they know the sources and chief interpretations; otherwise they would not know what to look for or where to find it, let alone how to frame assignments, discuss the material, or deal with students' comments. Teaching in this way also requires the imagination to work with diverse material and varied perspectives.

Work of this sort turns historical knowledge into a social resource for instruction, increases learners' opportunities to build bridges to

the material, and so is a move toward teaching practice. But it increases the difficulty and risks of instruction. As teachers extend instances of the Holocaust in many different voices or represent multiplication in several different ways, they diversify the range of ideas and experiences that they must master, and they complicate the issues with which they and students must deal. Teaching and learning are more complex when teachers introduce different or divergent accounts of events. If the past speaks in many voices, teachers and learners confront difficult problems of historical truth: were German citizens who lived near Auschwitz correct to claim that they knew of no executions? Faced with such puzzles, students, like historians, often wonder what really happened and what they can know.

If teachers extend knowledge in this way, they increase uncertainty and difficulty for themselves and their students. They must have the courage to manage uncertainty and the patience to work through complicated material. They must be daring enough to extend knowledge in ways that increase students' difficulty, even though that can increase the risk of failure or resistance. Expertise is never enough in teaching of any sort, and teaching in this way requires more supplements to knowledge and skills.

That helps explain why many teachers extend knowledge in less taxing ways. To use finished knowledge of facts and procedures (cell 1), teachers need only present strings of causes and effects, names and dates, and procedures and facts, and students need only reproduce them. Teachers can relatively easily make connections with learning because knowledge is clearly defined, and many students prefer that.[8] Teachers who work in this way need not know the material deeply, and even if they do, they need not deploy it; uncertainty and dispute are constrained, and teachers' dependence on students is limited.

There are alternatives between these extremes. One that is common in higher education is to treat knowledge as the result of inquiry but to extend it synoptically (cell 2). Some elementary-school teachers follow roughly the same path; they see mathematics as a matter of disciplined argument about quantity and shape and give special stress to problem setting and defense of results. They are keen that students learn about the intellectual structure of mathematics, but they extend the knowledge in polished and compressed form. A teacher might begin the 12 × 12 problem discussed earlier by saying:

> Whole-number multiplication procedures are just a way to combine equal groups of numbers. We could thus reformulate the 12 × 12 problem this way: How to combine twelve groups of twelve each? Problems of this sort could be solved by repeated addition, but that is quite inefficient unless the numbers are quite small. Multiplication is more efficient. Adding $x + x + x + x + x + x + x + x$ (however many times it is specified in y) is thus condensed and transformed into writing $x(y)$.
>
> But to multiply with two-digit numbers, one also must understand how numbers are put together in a system of place value. When we are doing the first step in this problem (multiplying 2 × 12), the multiplier, 2, is from the ones place in 12, while the multiplicand, 12, is from the tens. Hence multiplying 2 × 12 actually combines two different multiplications: 2 × 2 and 10 × 2. In the problem's second step—multiplying what looks like 1 × 12—one actually multiplies 10 by 12. The result of that operation is 120. Although one drops the zero in writing the second partial product, we recognize it by placing the product as though the zero were written. This convention reflects the fact that in

two-digit multiplication the second partial product is always in the hundreds. The last zero need not be written, but the product must be set one place to the left of the first partial product.

This version of multiplication is as synoptic as the earlier procedural example, but the two synopses contain different versions of mathematical knowledge. The first presents procedures as the core of mathematics, while the second offers a thoughtful account of how procedures work, and why. The first is far from the practice of mathematical inquiry because only a few products of inquiry are presented; the second is closer, for learners hear sophisticated reasoning, yet have few opportunities to do the work for themselves and thus engage with the ideas.

Some history instructors also extend finished interpretations rather than inviting students to weigh the evidence and frame and defend their own interpretations. Such teaching is no less synoptic than the earlier compressed narrative, but the content differs. One version offers the Holocaust as a thin string of dates, places, and events, while the second presents a dense set of ideas about what happened and what it means. Teachers commonly refer to both as explanations of history, but the nature of explanation differs radically: in the first case it is a compressed chronology, while in the second it is a finished argument.[9] The latter is a much richer example of historical argument, but the practice of historical inquiry—collecting and weighing evidence, making inferences about meaning and judgments about plausibility, generalizing from the evidence, and reaching conclusions—lies behind a veil of polished interpretation.

The second approach makes appreciable demands on teachers' knowledge, skills, and other resources because they must know much more than facts and procedures. It expands and complicates

instruction: when knowledge is construed as a matter of argument and interpretation, teachers grapple with complex ideas. The difficulty of teaching is greater because the knowledge extended is more uncertain, but that difficulty is limited because knowledge is not unpacked for learners to explore.[10] The synopses are much more complex than facts and procedures, but they remain compact and finished. This may strike observers as illogical, but the synopses widen the demands on teachers' personal resources and attentiveness in one dimension while constraining them in another.[11] Especially when teachers work in isolation, as most in the United States have done, managing the demands on one's personal resources has been especially useful because teachers have lacked many social resources that could support more ambitious work.

A rather different approach to knowledge extension is found among teachers who hold knowledge as fixed but extend it in unpacked form (cell 3). In teaching the 12 × 12 problem discussed above, instructors of this sort might combine tightly packed procedural expositions with varied representations. They might represent the procedures with groups of beans or sticks and invite students to use them; indeed, teachers may drill students in such representations, offering access to modestly unpacked versions of knowledge that are closely tied to drill and practice in procedures, rules, and facts. This approach offers somewhat expanded representations of multiplication within a view of arithmetical knowledge as fixed. Teaching of this sort seems increasingly to populate the instructional landscape as efforts to improve learning stimulate the development of new instructional materials and methods. The materials are designed on the view that knowledge is made, not received, and that students should explore a variety of representations, but the teachers who use these materials often consider knowledge fixed

and procedural. More and more elementary teachers use an array of graphic and concrete mathematical materials, but the materials do not seem to alter teachers' view of mathematics. They often treat the novel materials as procedures, much as they treat number problems on a worksheet.[12] Developers of the materials see such work as inconsistent and perverse, but many teachers report that the materials are helpful, in part because they engage students.

Knowledge that is extended in this fashion somewhat expands the demands on teachers' knowledge, skills, and other resources and moves teachers' performance toward a practice of teaching because they devise academic tasks and use representations that make knowledge more of a social resource and thus offer more opportunities for learners to gain access to knowledge. Although those varied representations are likely to provoke students' questions, teachers who use the materials in this way may only be able to respond with facts and procedures. The materials contain the potential for a richer version of arithmetic, but teachers often lack the knowledge to capitalize on the opportunities that the materials can create.

One thread in this account concerns the relation between teaching and fields of intellectual inquiry. When teachers extend thin and mechanical synopses of knowledge, they work at a great remove from the ways in which knowledge is produced, criticized, and revised. Such teaching offers learners a few fruits of others' inquiry and constrains the demands on teachers' knowledge, skills, and other personal resources, but it is unlikely to help students learn the skills of inquiry in which knowledge is produced. In contrast, some teaching invites learners to work as novices in creating, contesting, and reconstructing knowledge. Instead of tell-

ing inherited truths, teachers extend knowledge in ways that can help students cultivate the capacity to establish knowledge and learn how it is established, why it might be contested, and how those contests might be decided. That richer instructional diet offers learners more opportunities, but it also makes much greater demands on teachers' and learners' knowledge, skills, and other resources.

A second thread has been that the lack of teachers' efforts to unpack knowledge thoughtfully is no simple oversight that can easily be remedied by a bit of supplementary instruction. To extend knowledge in unpacked form cuts against the ways in which we learn and hold knowledge, and the value that we attach to polished performance. Much deliberate relearning and significant social resources would be required to enable good performers in any field to understand novice work and to learn how to identify and use the paths that would help beginners move toward competent performance. Recovering the elements of early and inexpert performance and learning instructional approaches that could help novices improve would entail much study of learning. Understanding how knowledge can be unpacked and extended to learners would require much analysis of knowledge and teaching, because such work is unnatural. Teachers also would need to have many opportunities to cultivate intellectual courage and adventurousness in order for them to learn to extend knowledge in ways that increased uncertainty and multiplied the difficulty of instruction.

To do such work, teachers would have to acquire a sort of double vision about knowledge: they would have to distance themselves from their own finished knowledge in order to extend what they know in more various and less finished ways, but they would have to use finished knowledge to guide and inform that teaching. Learn-

ing to hold and use knowledge in these different ways at the same time is essential for cultivating a sophisticated practice of teaching, but it is no mean feat.

The last thread in my discussion has been the great variation in how teachers build bridges toward learners, depending on how they hold knowledge and extend it. What counts as knowledge, a representation, or a connection among ideas varies dramatically, depending on how teachers construe knowledge and extend it. What teachers must know and what they must do in order to extend knowledge also vary. One result of that variation is that there has been nothing approaching a single body of expertise or technique in this occupation. What some commentators refer to as the "technical core" of education varies with the ways in which teachers hold ideas and extend them to learners, among other things. Therefore there has been no uniform technology of instruction or any single body of "essential" knowledge and skills for teaching. Instead, there are different possible bodies of knowledge and skills and varying degrees of overlap among them, depending on how teachers construe knowledge and extend it. It is difficult to see how the situation could have been otherwise, given deep differences about the nature of knowledge, continuing uncertainty and dispute about the ends and means of instruction, and the weak infrastructure and remarkably fragmented nature of schooling in the United States.

This situation is not carved in stone. In Chapter 4, I argued that it is possible to develop common expertise and techniques in systems of schools if there is a well-developed infrastructure and attention to how teachers and learners use it. If there were a common curriculum, common examinations keyed to that curriculum, and teacher education that focused on learning to teach that curriculum, educators would have the wherewithal to build common occupational

knowledge. If they did so, they could deepen and enrich teachers' knowledge and skills, limit variability in teaching, and make it possible for teachers to work in a system that supported coherent teaching practice.

That is roughly what several of the Comprehensive School Reform Designs and charter networks that I discussed in Chapter 4 have begun to do, and I noted there is substantial evidence that teaching in these systems is more effective for learners, less varied, and more consistent than in schools more generally. The sorts of variation that I have discussed in this chapter are endemic in teaching, but they do not express immutable differences in individuals' knowledge, skills, and dispositions. Instead, they express interactions between persistent predicaments of teaching and the existing social organizations of the occupation; the variation reflects both the social resources that are available to teachers and their individual attributes. If the social resources of teaching were different, teaching could be different.

6

INSTRUCTIONAL DISCOURSE

Knowledge is essential for instruction, but it is not enough. It becomes part of instruction when it joins a discourse in which learners encounter teachers and content. Instructional discourse is a socially organized means to extend and exchange knowledge, and it takes many different forms; lectures and small group discussions are only two examples.[1] Some consist of direct social interaction (for example, conventional lectures or discussions), but others are indirect interactions (for example, televised lectures, correspondence courses, distance learning, and computer networks). In the first kind, learners and teachers encounter each other face-to-face, but in the second, learners encounter teachers as pictures on a television screen, disembodied voices, instructional designs, comments on paper, words on a computer screen, and the like.

As these examples imply, instructional discourses depend not only on social organization but also on communication technologies, which also vary remarkably. In conventional direct discourse there are voices, books and paper, and chalk and blackboards, but more recent and less conventional indirect discourses depend on computers, and there may or may not be voices. Socrates' technology was as modest as the social organization of his teaching, but

computer networks require elaborate electronic technology to support forms of social organization that allow participants to disregard conventional limits of distance and time. Some recent innovations blur the line between direct and indirect discourse—Skype is one example—because they enable real-time video and audio interaction at great distances.

Social organization and technology are important because they shape learners' and teachers' participation in instruction. Discussion can enhance participation, but lectures typically constrain it; the short-wave radio networks once used in distance learning restricted learners' opportunity to participate, but recent computer networks can enhance it. Learners' participation is critical for several reasons. One is that the more they participate, the greater their chances to encounter, probe, and respond to what teachers and other learners offer, and, if participation is done well, they have more opportunities to improve their understanding. Another is that the more learners participate and shape instruction, the more opportunities teachers have to make connections with learning. Teachers who organize discourse in ways that increase learners' opportunities to participate increase their chances to cultivate a practice of teaching. Still another is that as learners' participation grows, teachers' opportunities to create social resources of practice also grow because their access to students' work and ideas can provide materials with which to enrich instruction. But participation can have a price: as it grows and connections between teaching and learning multiply, so do the complexity and uncertainty of instructional discourse and the demands on learners' and teachers' knowledge, skills, and other resources.

The conduct of instructional discourse has been hotly debated for nearly the entire history of the American experiment. Many teachers, pastors, and public officials in the seventeenth and eigh-

teenth centuries contended that teachers should dominate instruction because they were repositories of established knowledge, God's messengers, delegates of the adult community, agents of the state, or some combination of these. Instruction should model obedience to secular authority or divine power, deference to the wisdom of elders, or both. They believed that discourse taught as much by its form as by its content, and they championed teachers' dominance in the discourse; absent that dominance, students would learn things that would erode authority, social order, and a sense of man's proper place in the chain of being. Worries about Russian ambitions or Japanese cars were far in the future, but the politics of classroom work was a high-stakes matter even then.

Horace Mann, Bronson Alcott, and John Dewey agreed that students' participation in instruction was critical and, like their conservative adversaries, saw instructional discourse as both a model of and preparation for social relations. They opposed traditional practice and contended that students would suffer if they did not participate actively. Dewey made the case partly on the grounds that humans learned best by doing, by reconstructing knowledge rather than memorizing the finished results of what others had learned. Learning worked best when instruction was organized to support students' active engagement with one another in academic tasks.[2] Mann, Alcott, and others made the case partly on moral grounds: if students were to become responsible members of a community, they must learn responsibility early, through cooperative work and play. If teachers took charge of learning, students would expect others to take charge of them later on and would not learn moral independence.[3] Horace Mann used both arguments and, with other nineteenth-century educators, made a political case for participation: if students learned to cultivate critical

Table 6.1. Social organization, instructional discourse, technology, and participation

	Indirect discourse		Direct discourse	
	(1) Monologues (lectures)	(2) Dialogues (serial or simultaneous discussion)	(3) Monologues (lectures)	(4) Dialogues (recitation, discussion, interactive lectures)
Technology	Voice, books, tapes, computer-based instruction, radio or television broadcasts.	Two-way radio in distance education, two-way television, interactive computer networks, correspondence courses.	Voice, blackboard, paper.	Voice, blackboard, paper.
Participation	Learners watch, listen, or read. They have little direct influence on instructors.	Learners interact with teachers. The more interactive the technology, the more opportunity there is to participate in and shape instruction.	Learners and teachers interact face-to-face. Participation is usually limited, and learners have little direct influence on instruction.	Learners and teachers interact face-to-face. Learners can directly influence instruction.

Note: This table presents clear cases, but of course in reality types of instructional discourse often blur and overlap.

intelligence in circumstances that fostered mutual respect, they would acquire the crucial democratic virtues. It became common for educators in the mid- and late nineteenth century to refer to classrooms as "little republics" and to extol the importance of democratic participation in them. Finally, some commentators made the case for student participation in instructional discourse on philosophical grounds. Israel Scheffler argued that if the purpose of education is to encourage rationality, teachers who tell students everything will defeat education as they do it. Teachers can advance learning by engaging students in rational discourse, not by telling them what to think.[4]

This debate illustrates why Americans attach such importance to instructional discourse, what some of the issues are, and how Americans have argued about them. But it tells us little about what actually influences participation in instructional discourse, and what discourse entails for teachers and students.

Types of Instructional Discourse

I begin by distinguishing between direct and indirect interaction and between monologue and dialogue. Table 6.1 displays these types in the columns, the instruments and technologies that are used in the middle row, and the effects on communication and participation in the bottom row. Social organization and technology mediate instruction in all discourses, but they do so differently. Instruction in indirect interactive discourse (columns 1 and 2) is enabled by radio or television, computer networks, conventional mail, or other instruments and means of communication, while in direct discourse instruction is enabled by voice and other more traditional instruments.

Both discourse organization and instruments of communication shape opportunities for participation and for teachers to make connections with learning, but they set rather broad limits. The lowest row of the table sketches variation in the opportunities for learners' participation. Both direct and indirect monologues (columns 1 and 3) restrict opportunities to participate, but students are less constrained in direct than indirect monologues, and they are less constrained in indirect monologues by interactive computer networks than by correspondence courses. But technology and social organization are not all-powerful; how participants use them counts. Face-to-face lectures can be monologues or interactive, depending on what teachers and students do. Organization and technology create different opportunities for discourse, but they do not control what teachers and students do with those opportunities.

Moreover, learners' influence on instruction is quite extensive, even when they work alone on monologues that teachers produce alone. However carefully and independently teachers compose texts, lectures, or computer instruction, learners recompose them as they apprehend them. Many texts offer an overview of a field and focus on big ideas, but some students take them as detailed gospel rather than a guide to thought; they turn the big ideas into a mechanical collection of tidy memorized bits despite the authors' design. Other learners reshape texts and lectures by reading or listening inattentively; they learn something from paragraphs randomly scanned or sentences occasionally read as they watch television, listen to the radio, send text messages, talk with friends, or daydream. Or they read every third sentence or omit topics that they find boring. Some boys may reject elements of a history text or lecture because they give much attention to women's work, and some Catholics may ignore much in a medieval history lecture because it

does not accord with their beliefs. In these cases and others, learners reshape monologues as they learn from them, even though they do not literally rewrite the material.

Every instructional discourse is thus jointly and socially constructed, even if it is the work of one solitary soul on a desert island as he responds to a monologue produced by a hermit in a far-away closet. No learner sees in a text or hears in a lecture just what its author intended. By the same token, no teacher can imagine everything that learners may find in his or her texts or lectures, for that would require omniscience. Because no teacher has that capability, no one can anticipate students' many readings of his or her work, let alone take all possible steps to deal with them. At a minimum, learners participate in and shape instruction by the varied ways they apprehend and appropriate it. That is not direct interactive participation, but it is influential participation.

Indirect Discourse

There is thus a rather high lower limit on learners' influence on instruction. The chief point about indirectly interactive monologues (Table 6.1, column 1) is that learners cannot exceed that limit; however vigorously they attend to a text, a film, a televised lecture, or a computer program, and however varied their separate constructions may be, each learner works alone on monologues that teachers produce alone. Learners influence their own apprehension of the monologues, but they cannot influence what the teacher or other learners apprehend. Hence teachers have no opportunity to explain, correct, or revise instruction in light of students' responses, and no learner can be influenced by what the teacher or other learners say or do in response to a comment or question. Learners who work in

such monologues construct instruction jointly with their teachers, but serially and indirectly. Teachers speak or write to unknown and unseen students in various one-way technologies: printed texts, broadcast lectures, mailed tape cassettes, and the like. The demands on teachers' resources are relatively limited: they need to know the material they write or speak about, and they need some knowledge and skills of knowledge extension, but they need little interactive expertise because there is no direct social interaction. Hence they also need few supplements to knowledge and skills. If they are so inclined, they can construct a sophisticated practice of teaching with respect to knowledge extension while attending little to instructional discourse. As a consequence, teachers cannot create social resources of instruction additional to the monologue, and students cannot create such resources beyond their apprehension of the monologue.

Even a slight increase in the complexity of technology can appreciably increase learners' opportunities to participate. When teachers and students exchange taped or written lessons in distance learning programs or correspondence courses, the technology limits them to dyadic relations. Teachers may extend knowledge toward students in complex and sophisticated ways, but each teacher interacts with one student at a time. Teachers and students often wait for days and sometimes weeks to get responses to each piece of work they have assigned or completed. Possibilities for interaction are rather limited, but even these tutorials-at-a-distance open up more opportunities for students' participation and influence than solitary monologues. Teachers who read and comment on students' work through correspondence or distance learning programs can make more connections with learning than those who launch monologues into a void from which there can be no response. Students who can

scribble a note about their puzzles or tape-record a message about a point of curiosity have opportunities to influence instruction that are denied to those who merely read or listen to teachers. Teachers who work in even modestly interactive discourses have limited opportunities to interact with learners, but they have more than colleagues who extend monologues.

Other seemingly slight differences in technology produce similar gains in opportunities to participate. Teachers and students once worked in distance learning programs by using short-wave radio to supplement written lessons and mailed comments. Like correspondence, short-wave radio communication is limited because teachers speak to only one student at a time, and only one person can speak at a time. Such voice communication nonetheless offers students opportunities to participate and influence instruction because they can put a question directly to their teacher when it comes up rather than scribbling a note or recording a tape, mailing it, and waiting. In such cases teachers have more opportunities to make connections with learning. But each increase in the complexity of communication technology increases the demands on teachers' personal resources; those who exchange taped lessons or use short-wave radio require more interactive skill and knowledge than those who extend monologues.

Thus far I have considered technologies that permit communication on only one channel—voice or writing. But advances in computing now make it possible to link teachers in indirect interactions with many distant students at once. Computer networks can support voice and video communication, and multichannel communication greatly adds to students' capacity to participate and to influence instruction. If twenty students in different remote locations work on a computer network, their questions and comments

offer greater opportunities to influence instruction than if they worked individually on short-wave radio. Their collective participation can generate more material for consideration because in addition to each student making her own sense of texts and lectures, all students can share their views and understandings with the teacher, one another, or both. The capacity for such complex interaction increases students' potential influence on the pace, direction, and content of discourse, in part because of their increased intellectual output, but also in part because social pressures are stronger than in dyadic radio communications.[5] Communication technology of this sort also enhances teachers' capacities to make connections with learning. Even at a distance they are able to see students' work, hear them explain it, comment on one another's ideas, put questions, and get answers. This presents teachers with material that they can use to fashion social resources of instruction that would be impossible in dyadic relations. One example is turning one student's question back to the group and asking for comments. Another is collecting several students' comments on a text and using them to frame further discussion. In these cases and others, even indirect interactive discourse makes it possible to use participation to build social resources of instruction.

Recent technical advances enable rich indirect discourses that are relatively unconstrained by space and time. As technologies support more complex interactions, such learning communities will exhibit more features of direct instructional discourse.[6] Teachers' opportunities to make connections with learning also increase with greater technical sophistication. Teachers who work in correspondence courses interact with students intermittently at a great distance and have limited chances to respond to students' work, but teachers who interact with students on computer networks have

more opportunities to see students' work and respond. Because they can know more about students' work and have more chances to connect with it, they have more of the wherewithal to construct a practice of teaching, even if the students are far removed.[7]

But these connections and opportunities come at a price. The more complex indirect discourse becomes, the more demands it makes on teachers' expertise and other personal resources. New technologies may enable remarkable new forms of instruction, but the more connections and influence that teachers seek, the more they must interact with students, and the more they interact, the more opportunities students have to act back and influence instruction. One advantage of monologues is that teachers can work without opening themselves to students' influence. That restricts teachers' opportunities to make connections with learners and it limits learning, but it simplifies teaching. Teachers who open discourse to more interaction increase their chances to influence students, but only by increasing students' opportunities to return the favor.

Direct Discourse

Technology shapes participation and influence in indirect discourse by defining the nature and extent of social interaction. But when students and teachers meet face-to-face, the mediating instruments are voice, vision, books, papers, and pencils, and social organization is the chief constraint on communication and mutual influence. Unlike technology, social organization is something that students and teachers can shape. Discussion is a discourse organization that opens opportunities for students' and teachers' participation and mutual influence, but it requires considerable instructional knowledge and skill. Other forms of discourse organization,

such as seatwork (when students work individually and ordinarily silently, at their desks), constrain participation and opportunities for mutual influence and thus constrain the instructional skills and knowledge that students and teachers must cultivate.

Table 6.2 identifies several forms of direct discourse and summarizes a few of their key features. Individual seatwork (column 1) has perhaps the greatest potential to restrict interaction about

Table 6.2.   Types of direct instructional organization and implications for discourse

A. Types of organization

(1) Seatwork	(2) Lecture	(3) Recitation	(4) Discussion
Instructors can monopolize discourse. Whole-class work is virtually eliminated. Teachers speak chiefly with individuals, and most communication is written. Most instruction is private.	Instructors usually monopolize discourse. They speak to everyone, but no one need respond; students are an audience. Discourse is public.	Instruction is public and students participate, but they speak in response to teachers. Students help create discourse, but on teachers' terms.	Instructors and students share participation. If discussion is well done, students express their views and questions and speak to one another, as well as to the teacher.

B. Effects on discourse

(1) Seatwork	(2) Lecture	(3) Recitation	(4) Discussion
Students' chances to influence discourse directly are quite limited.	Students usually have limited direct influence on discourse.	Students have modest chances to influence discourse directly.	If discussion is well done, students can have large direct influence on discourse.

subject matter and thus to limit students' participation and influence. Students may resist it for this reason, but if they acquiesce, they work individually on assignments set by a teacher. The class is atomized, and discourse is privatized; teachers only intermittently interact with students and then individually, if students come to their desk or teachers walk around checking work. Many interactions are indirect—for example, directions for assignments are written, and papers are corrected in writing and returned without spoken comment. Teaching consists in making and managing assignments and issuing directions and corrections; learning consists in following directions, doing assignments, and often even correcting them—each in isolation. There is little public activity that students might affect.

Seatwork reduces students' chances for public interaction within instruction and so reduces their opportunities to distract and disrupt in that sphere. It also reduces the opportunity to create social resources for instruction. But precisely because discourse is privatized, seatwork creates many opportunities for participation outside instruction, such as reading, passing notes, whispering, walking to the wastebasket or the pencil sharpener, and the like. When the public sphere of instruction is so dramatically narrowed, its borderland expands and creates opportunities for additional interaction around the fringes. These actions in the borderland can shape instruction by distracting from it, slowing it down, or derailing it, even though they rarely can exert much direct effect on the content of instruction.[8]

Lectures (column 2) also usually restrict interaction and thus restrain students' participation and influence, but the dynamic is different. Because lectures are public and directed at a group, they do not atomize classes and privatize speech. Restriction of interaction and influence arise instead if lecturers monopolize public

speech. If they do, students are treated as an audience. Audiences receive and regard, but they do not perform or produce. Lectures can free instructors by restricting auditors' participation and influence, but that restriction creates freedom for auditors; if lecturers monopolize discourse and shrink students' direct participation, the instructional borderland expands, creating opportunities for students to read, sleep, pass notes, or whisper, all around the edges of the monologue. If students acquiesce in lectures, they have little room to influence the form or content of discourse directly, but ample room to operate in the borderland. Those operations seem to be independent of instruction, but they can affect it indirectly by distracting or derailing instructors or distracting students' attention.

Discussion (column 4) is less restrictive. If it is skillfully done, students can shape the discourse in direct interaction among themselves and with teachers by arguing, explaining, and questioning. When discussion works, students teach and learn from one another, as well as from teachers. If they do not play a large public part, discussion cannot work; learners must produce much of the instruction in order to learn. Discussion also offers teachers many opportunities to make connections with learning because what students make of instruction is vividly presented. That, in turn, offers teachers and students material with which to fashion additional social resources of instruction.

Teachers often find it risky to organize discourse in this way because it creates opportunities for students to stop the music with a puzzling comment, to alter the agenda, or to disrupt the class. Students have few such opportunities in lectures and seatwork, and their chances to disrupt the class lie chiefly in the borderland. This disruption therefore must be controlled by "discipline," that is,

teachers' direct efforts to shape students' behavior apart from the content of instruction.[9] But if discussion works, it deals with potential disruption by expanding the public realm and shrinking the social space for private interaction. That constrains students' opportunities to interact privately on the fringes. If participation remains high and relevant, there is little other social space, and thus few "discipline" problems arise that teachers must manage apart from discussion.[10]

Formal recitation (column 3) is distinctive: students are expected to participate actively, often as much as in discussion, but teachers fix the schedule, content, and format. Teachers put the questions, and students answer. Students typically can neither question the questions nor argue the answers. They speak to the teacher, not to one another. The discourse is public but one-sided, a fascinating combination of public and private interaction. It resembles seatwork in that communication usually pairs an individual student and a teacher, but it resembles discussion in that it is actively and jointly constructed; unlike lectures, recitation cannot work if students snooze or read, and it can give teachers considerable access to students' knowledge. Like discussion, if recitation works it reduces students' opportunities to interact privately around the margins of the discourse. One reason is that the discourse is public; unlike seatwork, other students are audience and potential participants. Another is that the incentives in recitation are different from those in seatwork because what the reciting student says is likely to have consequences for the next speaker, as in discussion. The next student's identity is often unknown, so it pays to listen. Hence when recitations work, attention is likely to focus on what class members say and do. Effective recitations also tend to be quite rapid and to require attention. All these factors narrow the

instructional borderland. But even though students participate actively, the discourse restricts their opportunities to influence both content and form. Thus recitations are a bargain for many teachers: they permit extensive student participation and thus help with discipline, but they constrain participation by allowing teachers to control its pace, content, and direction. This feature may help explain why this form of discourse has been so durable.

Discourse, Knowledge, and Instructional Resources

Thus far I have sketched several chief types of discourse, referred to the expertise and other resources that are entailed, and alluded to the opportunities to cultivate a practice of teaching in various discourses. But these issues cannot be satisfactorily explored with reference to discourse alone. Discourse exists to exchange knowledge. Therefore, to probe adequately what varied discourse organizations imply for teaching, I must consider them along with conceptions of knowledge.

Table 6.3 summarizes a few of the chief ways in which discourse forms can combine with versions of knowledge, and what the combinations entail for teaching and learning. Begin with the least demanding approaches: lectures, seatwork, and recitations in which teachers treat knowledge as fixed (cells 1, 2, and 3). These combinations are widely represented in school and university classrooms, partly because there is a good match between forms of discourse and conceptions of knowledge. Recitations and seatwork are easier to conduct if students can give crisp and simple answers, and those are well adapted to a view of knowledge as fixed. Also, if knowledge is treated as fixed, it seems reasonable that instructors should speak texts. Not surprisingly, teachers who use one of these approaches

Table 6.3. Interactions of discourse forms and knowledge conceptions and their implications for students' influence and teachers' knowledge

	Knowledge treated as fixed		
Seatwork	Lecture	Recitation	Discussion
(1) Students' participation in and effect on discourse is limited. They can probe the subject little. Instructors need few resources other than some knowledge of the subject.	(2) Students' participation in and direct effect on discourse is limited. There usually are few student probes of the subject. Instructors require few specialized resources other than some knowledge of the subject.	(3) Students' participation in and direct effect on discourse is limited. Instructors require some specialized resources other than subject knowledge, but students' probes of the subject are limited.	(4) Students' participation in and direct effect on discourse is greater. Instructors require more specialized resources to manage complex interactions, but students' probes of the subject are limited.
	Knowledge treated as the result of inquiry		
(5) Students' participation in and effect on discourse varies. Some teachers thoughtfully design solo work, while others press innovative views of knowledge into a stiff format. The skills and knowledge needed also vary.	(6) Students' participation in and effect on discourse usually is limited. Many lecturers assert that knowledge is constructed and contested but monopolize discourse. Much knowledge of subjects is needed, but less interactive skill.	(7) Students' participation in and effect on discourse usually is limited. Many teachers assert that knowledge is constructed and contested but use this format to interrogate students. Knowledge of subjects and interactive expertise are needed.	(8) Students' participation in and effect on discourse can be extensive. Teachers invite students to work as novice inquirers, and they employ various discussion formats. They need much subject-matter knowledge and interactive expertise.

often use another. Elementary-school teachers regularly combine recitation with seatwork; university instructors commonly combine lectures with recitations; and secondary-school teachers often use all three.

When teachers combine seatwork with a fixed conception of knowledge (cell 1), they constrain instructional discourse. Students fill in the blanks, answer multiple choice questions, solve set problems, and write short answers. Their responses are right or wrong. They interact individually with the teacher, but their opportunities to question, explain, argue, or even express puzzles about the subject are limited. This approach limits demands on teachers' instructional expertise; as long as students acquiesce, instructors need only modest knowledge and skills, including some knowledge of the subject, how to make or find worksheets, and how to correct them. Teachers require little specialized interactive skill because direct social interaction is circumscribed. The demands on students are similarly limited; they need not learn to speak plausibly and coherently about what they think or know, to explain or justify their ideas, or to challenge or comment on one another's ideas. Teachers need not learn how to evoke, sustain, and assess such discourse.

This sort of teaching might be seen as the face-to-face equivalent of simple distance or correspondence instruction, in which limited communication technology compels teachers and students to work mostly by themselves on fixed instructional agendas. But when such work is carried on in classrooms, it is not because there are technical barriers to direct interaction but because teachers and students organize social barriers. They structure discourse in a way that sharply restricts interaction, and they represent knowledge in ways that restrict intellectual interaction. Teaching of this sort has been common in U.S. public schools.

When teachers lecture and treat knowledge as fixed (cell 2), they also constrain the demands on their knowledge and skills. Their conception of knowledge limits the intellectual depth of discourse, and the discourse organization usually limits participation. If teachers monopolize the discourse, students have few opportunities to raise questions, explore puzzles, or challenge the instructor. Some high-school lecturers of this sort know the material only superficially, while many university lecturers are deeply knowledgeable, but both present knowledge as facts and formulas. Some use the same notes year after year, viewing and presenting their words as one might do with a written text. Little additional specialized knowledge and skills are required beyond knowledge of the material. Many lecturers in universities and secondary schools employ little more than ordinary knowledge of ordinary interaction, including the tact to begin and end more or less on time, to speak clearly, and perhaps to answer a few questions. Some university instructors further reduce the demands on their interactive skills by avoiding any interaction with students, leaving that to graduate assistants who teach discussion sections.

This approach can be seen as a face-to-face equivalent of broadcast radio or television classes, in which the teacher is a talking head. In distance learning of that sort, the technology restricts students' opportunities to participate and shape the discourse, as well as teachers' opportunities to influence students. But there are no technical barriers in lectures; the restrictions on participation and influence are socially constructed by teachers who work in this way and by students who accept it. Some lecturers cultivate a very sophisticated practice, but they are few and far between.

These two sorts of instruction tend to insulate teachers from the predicaments of human improvement. One reason is that they

constrain uncertainty. Students and teachers have little room to notice puzzles, problems, or ambiguities in their work because both the form of discourse and the conception of knowledge restrict opportunities to question and discuss. Another is that these restrictions on students' academic performance limit teachers' dependence. If lecturers turn teaching into something approaching solo performance, they depend on students to show up, listen, take notes, or at least not disrupt, but students need to do little else to sustain instruction. Teachers can lecture for a term without requiring anything of students save perhaps attendance.[11] Teachers can achieve a species of success without cultivating a practice of teaching. American universities and secondary schools abound with teachers who perform thus, teaching alone in the company of many students.

Recitations in which knowledge is treated as fixed (cell 3) are somewhat more demanding. Discourse is constrained because students interact with the teacher, serially and individually, but there is extensive interaction about the material. Teachers may pose scores of questions and mobilize broad student participation, but in a stylized discourse in which teachers question and students answer. Teachers decide on the questions and on timing. Students speak, but usually only when spoken to. Because teachers focus on right answers, they can carry on rapid-fire, rephrasing or ignoring complicated, partial, or confused answers.

It is no mean feat to manage such instruction well. Teachers require skill in managing a large group and perhaps the capacity to coax participation from reticent students while cooling it from their overeager mates. They cannot manage well without some command of both the material and discourse about it, including the

capacity to frame suitable questions, weigh the answers, and pace the activity. Public exploration of students' knowledge makes more demands on teachers' knowledge and skills than lectures and seatwork, even when the discourse and view of knowledge are tightly constrained, because when teachers query students' knowledge in public, they lack a key means to manage interaction if they cannot manage the knowledge.

Recitations of this sort increase problems of human improvement a bit. Uncertainty grows because calling on students in public increases the chance of unexpected problems, which are less likely in standard seatwork or lectures. Teachers' dependence increases because students must participate and answer questions if the class is to succeed. They also must answer a fair proportion correctly, for when students' knowledge is on public display, teachers depend on them much more visibly than in seatwork or lectures. A class that produces mostly wrong answers can be an embarrassment and in acute cases can even erode a teacher's authority. Therefore, if there are many incorrect answers, teachers may terminate a recitation. Correct answers are a sign not only of students' progress but also of successful teaching, and incorrect answers can be the reverse; students' performance is potentially more volatile because problems of knowledge can provoke problems of management. In this case, as in some others, when teachers' skills and knowledge are made more public, teachers become not only more visible but also more vulnerable. If recitations offer modestly greater opportunities to cultivate a practice of teaching than lectures or seatwork, they require more supplements to technical knowledge and skills, as when teachers must encourage students to study, to participate in the recitation, and to maintain civility.

Several other sorts of discourse combine ambitious teaching in one dimension with more cautious work in another. One is the use of open discussion while treating knowledge as fixed (cell 4). In such cases classroom conversation can be relaxed and free, but the content is rigid. In many U.S. elementary schools children work in small groups, talk easily with one another and the teacher, and move freely around the room; there seem to be few barriers to interaction about ideas. But the content over which teachers and students interact so flexibly is set out in mimeographed worksheets, word lists, pages of set problems, and the like. Classroom discourse is relaxed and open but also brief and superficial. A similar pattern prevails in many high-school classes: there is plenty of interaction, but the content is thin. Teachers often run "discussions" in which students serially offer views on a topic but do not engage one another's ideas. Teachers wait until the desired answer has been presented and then move on. If one watched on television and saw only the picture, these could seem like thoughtful discussions, but if one heard the sound, they would seem more like recitations.[12]

Alternatively, many teachers who profess that knowledge is the fruit of learners' inquiries offer pure monologues (cell 6). This kind of discourse organization is common in U.S. universities, where professors present inventive views of a topic but proceed as though they could construct knowledge for the students. One might dismiss this approach as inconsistent, but it is not irrational, because these teachers adopt an expansive vision of knowledge without also adopting a discourse organization that would embroil them in interacting with students' ideas. Such teachers advance ambitious aims for students while limiting their dependence on students' performance; they cultivate a sophisticated conception of knowledge without cultivating the discourse and the instruc-

tional knowledge and skills that could help many students follow suit.

Such seemingly inconsistent combinations often appear after the introduction of innovative curricula. Innovators persistently try to open academic discourse to new approaches to content and interaction, but teachers and students find it easier to adopt elements of flexible discourse organization without learning new conceptions of content. Despite the appearance of inconsistency, teachers can work in ways that embody appealing values while limiting the difficulty of such work, especially when they are not offered suitable opportunities to learn the new material. They combine a relatively sophisticated practice of teaching in one domain with a less difficult approach in another.

A similar case is that of teachers who conduct recitations in the standard form even though they profess to view knowledge as the product of learners' inquiry (cell 7). Although they invite more complex answers from students than teachers commonly do—an explanation of the evolutionary hypothesis, a description of the New Deal, or an account of what causes solar eclipses—there are limits on the responses that they will entertain. They ask for the answer that they proposed, or for the answer that they believe students can correctly construct. They search for answers, not accounts of various constructions, explanations of how students arrived at their views, or justifications of those views. Although they see knowledge as the product of learners' inquiry, their organization of discourse limits knowledge exchange with students.[13]

To appreciate these approaches, it helps to consider an alternative—teachers who use an open and participatory discourse in efforts to help students cultivate inquiries (cell 8). Consider a fourth-grade teacher whose students are beginning to study division. In order to

explore the mathematical ideas, she may invite the class to estimate the answer to a simple division problem—say, six into thirty—and to explain their estimates. Estimation can help students get a sense of the magnitudes involved, and discussion can generate some useful insights into division. If her class is at all typical, several students will say nothing, another may say that six "fits" into thirty twice, and another may say that it "goes" three times. Still another may go to the board and draw five groups of cats, with six in each group. My hypothetical teacher knows something about arithmetic and so is not floored by these varied ideas, but she may be puzzled. Six does "fit" into thirty twice, after all. It also fits three times, four times, and five times. How does one deal with a student who answers "two" or "three"? And how can she best capitalize on the blackboard drawing? But before she has time to decide, another student says that the answer is ten, and two others say five.

The teacher wants her students to make sense of arithmetic, so she invites them to explain their estimates. The student who said that six fit into thirty twice responds that $6 + 6 = 12$, that twelve is less than thirty, and so six fits into thirty twice. One student who gave the correct numerical answer writes the problem in standard form on the board but cannot explain how she got the answer; she learned it from her uncle, she reports. The student who answered "ten" cannot explain his answer either, but he is adamant that it is correct. The student who drew five groups of cats on the board says simply that "division is putting things into groups." And the other student who answered "five" writes a different problem—fifteen divided by three—on the board. He defends his answer by saying that his problem is "equal" to six into thirty.

This approach can begin a fruitful discussion. Quite a few students have responded to the teacher's invitation, produced a variety

of mathematically interesting ideas, and begun to explain them. Several answers suggest some insight into division, but of quite different sorts. One reveals mechanical knowledge of division as most adults see it, but no apparent understanding of the ideas. Two others hint at a greater grasp of division than many U.S. adults have, but they are unusual and in some respects divergent. There also are students with no apparent answers and one who seems to be in left field. The teacher wants this class to become a division-problem-solving-and-debating society, but how can she best help students create that society? Should she begin with the right answer, and if so, which one? The one that pictured division as groups of cats, or the one that offered a reduced-form version of the problem? Perhaps it would be more fruitful to begin with the students who said that six fit into thirty two and three times. There is something defensible in their point, and they may be closer to most of the class's view of the matter; perhaps that view will be more useful for the students who said nothing. But will it be useful for the students who offered the other ideas? Can they be kept in the discussion if a less sophisticated answer is taken up?

Teachers who take more traditional approaches to this part of arithmetic will have fewer puzzles. They may demonstrate how division is done in a lecture in which they go over the standard algorithm at the board (cell 2). They may hand out or dictate some problems and work with students as they practice and memorize the procedures (cell 1). They may conduct a recitation on division (cell 3). Or they may combine the three approaches. A knowledgeable teacher may expound on division in a lecture (cell 6) in which she represents different approaches to division, discusses conflict over the meaning of division, and explores uncertainty about which approach is best, all in her monologue. To do this she needs imagination, insight, and

a capacity for vivid expression, but she can manage everything herself, taking key ideas, disputes, and puzzles in the order and at the pace she thinks best. She can ask only the questions she thinks important, give the answers she thinks sufficient, and do so at the times she thinks appropriate. A teacher of this sort can clearly expose a topic or a field and build bridges toward students as she goes. This work is not easy: instructors must be knowledgeable about the material and skillful in unpacking it. But by expounding on it in a monologue, they constrain difficulty and uncertainty. By eliminating other participants, they close off unpredictable elements of a many-sided conversation and the skill and knowledge required to orchestrate it.

My hypothetical teacher will have to embrace those unpredictable elements if she aims to help students produce the discussion she wants (cell 8). She must manage complicated interactions, keep track of many difficult ideas, help regulate students' participation, and help students learn the conventions of the discourse and how to conduct themselves in it, all more or less at once. To do so, she must both appreciate the virtues of several seemingly contrary views of a problem and help students cultivate this appreciation in their work. Because there will be few occasions in which most students grasp anything the first time, she also must be able to encourage students to risk being wrong, to try to explain their ideas, and to figure out how to improve them. She must find ways to maintain the engagement of students who are quick and those who are not quick, and she must cope with students who hesitate, balk, or simply do not get it.

When instruction of this sort goes well, classrooms become little communities of inquiry, but it goes well only if teachers and students can manage complex ideas in complicated interactions. Teach-

ers must have a sophisticated command of a tradition of inquiry and argument and a thoughtful appreciation of how novices think about a body of material.[14] They must be quick to grasp an idea but patient in encouraging many ideas that are weakly expressed or tentatively advanced. They must understand the key elements in a field and be able to help a class weave arguments about them. To return to the division example above, teachers must blend their understanding of number groups and various ways of representing them with the imagination, tact, and patience to elicit students' ideas about how to divide and combine them, and how to represent these divisions and combinations. They must combine the mathematical knowledge required to help students sift through the ideas and distinguish those that are germane from those that are not with the capacity to minimize distraction, avoid hurt feelings, keep participation alive, and manage discussion of ideas and arguments. Any one of these qualities requires considerable skill and knowledge; together they require formidable expertise and many supplements to it. Teachers who do such work cultivate a complex and sophisticated practice of teaching.

The demands on students also are considerable. To invite them to understand division as my hypothetical teacher does is to delegate extensive responsibility for instruction to them. The student who said that division is "putting things into groups" may have to explain why he chose the groups he did. His classmate who solved the problem by dividing three into fifteen may have to explain and defend his approach. Most American adults who can "do" division cannot explain how it works, and few can make the explanations and defenses that I just mentioned. But my hypothetical teacher cannot succeed unless the students who produce mathematical inventions and represent their ideas imaginatively are thoughtful

and persistent in explaining and defending their ideas. Such work can be exciting, but it also can be tough. Some students revel in it, but others find it difficult. Even if they willingly make and correct many errors in privately prepared assignments, they prefer to present only polished work in public. Some can find such discussions difficult because they require an unusual combination of detachment and engagement; they must care enough to dig deeply into problems and work hard, and they must be sufficiently convinced of their ideas to expose them to classmates and champion them in discussion, but they must be tentative enough to entertain questions, consider alternative views, and revise their thinking. They must be both convinced and flexible. None of this is easy. Some never get started because they cannot engage their own ideas, while others have a surplus of engagement and cannot get enough distance to seriously entertain questions or revisions.[15] This should be no surprise, for many members of school and university faculties have difficulty accepting criticism of their work or tolerating others' ideas. Why should children or adolescents do better? Students often can work in this way only if they receive help in learning how to present their comments and reactions and how to work with others.

The sort of discourse sketched here entails an unusual intellectual and political order. In conventional classrooms teachers often justify their decisions by reference to the authority of a text or their position as the delegate of a state agency. Disputes about an answer can be settled peremptorily by reference to a page at the chapter's end. Disputes about how much to argue, or how, can be settled by telling a student to be quiet or by dispatching the offender from class. But when teachers help students create little "republics of science,"[16] they cannot settle disputes by referring to

a text or external authority, because they seek to create classrooms in which decisions about the worth of ideas rest on the quality of arguments and the plausibility of evidence; the more compelling students' arguments, the greater their authority, and the fuller their partnership in instruction. If such classes succeed, they do so partly because teachers decrease reliance on the traditional instruments of authority in order to help students develop their authority and influence. Students more fully coproduce instruction, not in the sense of absorbing what teachers say but in the sense of teaching one another and guiding the class's work. The more teachers succeed in such work, the more they implicate learning in teaching.

Such teaching heightens predicaments of human improvement. Uncertainty becomes central to instruction, in part because the explanation and justification of ideas open up different ways to think about issues and make those differences central to the class's work. My hypothetical arithmetic teacher multiplies uncertainty about what happens in division, what it means, and how best to represent it; discussing the competing ideas sheds light on this part of arithmetic, but it does so by exploring differences of opinion and obscurities in the conventional algorithm. Uncertainty also increases because students' participation increases. Teachers have a good deal of student commentary to attend to, some of it puzzling, and they must make many decisions about the conduct of instruction. Since the 1950s U.S. social scientists have pictured the human mind as deeply averse to uncertainty and searching for ways to reduce it, but this sort of teaching works only when teachers and students embrace and capitalize on uncertainty.

Teachers' dependence on students also increases. My hypothetical arithmetic teacher cannot succeed unless her students become

practiced mathematical inventors, debaters, and explainers. They must think on their feet, defend their ideas, and criticize others' ideas in the open arena of the class, where everyone can see and hear how well they are doing. This sort of discourse requires such public work. When students do it well, the result is remarkable, but when they do not do well, the consequences are hung out for all to see. Because teachers' work is so closely and publicly identified with students' work in such classes, it is difficult to avoid the conclusion that teachers have not done well when students do not. One virtue of seatwork is that it attenuates the connections between teachers' and students' work and thereby eases teachers' dependence. Teachers depend on students only to fill in their worksheets, remember algorithms, and work problems, and little work is public. Some teachers excel at the sort of discussions that I sketched, but others, no less committed to students' reasoning, find it unsettling to stake their own success so heavily on students' public performance. Some cope by conducting discussions themselves, asking questions and answering them while students sit quietly by. Others find the mere prospect of wrong answers, no answers, or listless discussions so troubling that they retreat into the safe solitude of lectures.

Teaching and learning of this sort are rare, in part because they depend heavily on the resources that students and teachers bring to and mobilize in the class. Teachers who work in this way may do so in schools in which few colleagues work in similar ways, and in which students therefore have little experience with such instruction apart from one unusual class. If so, teachers and students have limited opportunities to learn how to conduct such instruction, and they have little or no support for the work apart from what they can muster in the class in question. If stu-

dents had such opportunities in most of their academic work, their facility would improve, and if teachers worked in schools in which most of their colleagues taught in similar ways, they would have more social resources of instruction with which to work.

When teachers and students work in school systems that organize social resources to improve instruction, as a few comprehensive school reform designs and charter networks have done, teachers have access to colleagues who can support their classroom work. One example is grade-level conferences in which teachers study work that their students have done, and help one another figure out what it means and how to improve teaching and learning. Such conferences can model the sorts of discussion that teachers try to organize in their classrooms, and in this way and others they mobilize social resources that support instruction. But such resources are simply absent in most schools in the United States, and that helps explain why many teachers are unable to carry through demanding work that they begin, and why many others choose much less ambitious approaches to instructional discourse.

One thread in my analysis concerns the relations between two different sorts of resources that practitioners can deploy: (1) their specialized knowledge and skills and (2) alternatives to knowledge and skills. Some instructional approaches depend heavily on such alternatives. When students work alone at their desks, the discourse organization restricts teachers' need for instructional expertise by atomizing the class. Individual students work alone, and most communication is between single students and the teacher. Teachers' knowledge of subject matter may be

specialized but need not be; once the organization is in place, the demands on instructors' personal resources can be modest. Lectures often function in a similar way; organizing discourse as the instructor's monopoly can greatly reduce the other knowledge and skills that might be required in more interactive formats. In these cases relatively simple organizational devices substitute for the extensive instructional skills and knowledge that are required in other types of discourse.

In contrast, instructional discourse of the sort illustrated by my earlier example of teaching division greatly increases the demands on teachers, in part because the capabilities seem almost contrary: despite possessing expert knowledge about their subject, teachers must be expert at holding their tongues and encouraging others, much less expert, to contribute and learn. Such work is quite unusual and, given the nature of most instructional discourse, it seems fair to term it unnatural. I do not mean that it is impossible—it is entirely possible—but it departs so sharply from conventional instructional discourse that teachers and students have a great deal to learn to manage it well. Teachers must be more knowledgeable than in other approaches to instructional discourse, but they must be especially knowledgeable about designing instruction that takes them out of the spotlight and puts students in it. Teachers who work in this way depend on students to do much more than usual, but their students can only do more if teachers do and know more than usual. One might think that teachers would become less responsible for instruction and less vulnerable as students become more responsible, but the more teachers help students make instruction an active joint creation, the more they depend on students' performance, and the more adept students must be as novice mathematicians, historians, or commentators

on literature. Teachers must become unusually adept and knowledgeable in order to make themselves unusually vulnerable. Individual teachers can cultivate these qualities in the isolation that has been pervasive in U.S. schools, but they are less difficult to cultivate in schools and school systems that mobilize social resources to support such work.

7

TEACHERS' ACQUAINTANCE WITH STUDENTS' KNOWLEDGE

Teaching and learning are two distinct practices. Though they are often related, often they are not. How they are related and how closely depend partly on how teachers and students regulate the connections. I discussed two domains for that regulation in chapters 5 and 6: some approaches to extending knowledge or organizing discourse increase the opportunities to connect teaching and learning, while others reduce them. Teachers' acquaintance with students' knowledge is the third domain.[1] The more teachers learn about what students know, the more learning can be implicated in teaching, and the more sophisticated the practice that teachers can devise; but the less they learn about students' knowledge, the less teachers need take learning into account, and the freer they are to teach as they like, or are able.

Teachers are not alone in attending to others' knowledge. We all do so in all sorts of discourse. We intermittently check on whether we are understood in conversation, and even in monologues we try to make ourselves plain to some unknown other. Most of this concern with others' understanding is cultivated entirely with the ordinary knowledge of everyday life. We employ simple syntax or the

local vernacular, or we vary our vocabulary to suit the auditor. We probe a point, pause in midsentence with an inquiring glance, or ask a fragmentary question. We proceed in light of what people say, the looks on their faces, or what we fancy they think. Some give much time to this matter, learning to put themselves in others' mental shoes, while others give little. Some excel at making themselves understood, designing what they say in light of what auditors are likely to know or expect, while others do poorly. But whether people do little or much, well or poorly, few cultivate specialized skill or technical knowledge in their efforts to understand others or make themselves understood.

Because teachers' task is to make matters understood, they cannot avoid adopting some stance toward students' knowledge, but their stances vary enormously. Some create what seems to them an intelligible discourse and barely attend to what students make of it, while others closely investigate students' knowledge and try to teach in ways that respond to what they hear from students and see in their work. But even teachers who attend to students' knowledge do so very differently. Some devote much time to the matter, while many others devote little. The differences do not end there; even among those who devote much time to discerning what students know, some make sophisticated efforts and cultivate considerable skills of inquiry, while others make crude efforts and use only ordinary knowledge and skills.

Teachers' attention to students' knowledge is part of an old American argument about the connections between teaching and learning. New England's original Calvinists allocated much time to teaching scripture, prayer, and related matters, and they had little doubt that they could know what was in most minds: sinful thoughts, resistance to divine will, and worse. But they did not believe that teaching

would help most sinners, for they saw grace rather than human action as decisive.

This unforgiving creed had a relatively brief career; by the late eighteenth century some educated Americans adopted a more hopeful view of teaching and learning. Thomas Jefferson, Thomas Paine, and others asserted that the mind was formed by its circumstances, and that what people knew resulted from sense data impressed on their minds from without. If the mind was neutral or plastic, as these men believed, it was easy to think that learning would be sensitive to teaching. Like other Enlightenment thinkers, Jefferson and his fellows deplored ignorance and suspicion, but they thought it the result of bad instruction by churches and despots. If teaching were enlightened, humanity would follow suit.

Those ideas were reinforced by a uniquely easy and optimistic populist Protestantism that swept much of the Northeast and Midwest in the early nineteenth century. Baptists, Methodists, and others asserted that learning was natural; they saw children as innocent rather than depraved, and human nature as either inherently good or so little bad as to be easily corrected. In the more popular Protestant sects it was believed that anyone could teach and minister if he was gently disposed and saved. The difficulties of investigating what students learned did not play a large part in this line of thought and practice because these Americans saw learning as so natural that students would be receptive to any decent instruction.

In both secular and Protestant traditions of thought, human improvement thus was seen as easy because humanity was seen as impressionable, inherently good, or both. Educators assumed that teaching and learning could be connected: as long as teachers offered decent lessons, students would learn. If minds were so open to influence, there was no need to adapt teaching to learning,

because learning would so easily be shaped by teaching. Educators and reformers sometimes seemed to see learning as a copy of teaching and to believe that the solution to many educational problems lay in changing the content of teaching; investigating what students learned was much less important than teaching what they should learn. These views also led social reformers then and later to see instruction as a virtual cure-all; they could remedy any problem simply by teaching people how to think, what to believe, and how to act. If people learned what they were taught, social problems could be solved.

A few elements of this faith were contested. Early in the nineteenth century several critics began to attack the idea that children would learn anything they were taught. They argued that children thought differently than adults and that teachers should adapt instruction accordingly. One early dissenter was Warren Colburn, an enterprising 1820s textbook author who wrote the first version of the new math.[2] Another was Bronson Alcott, an ardent utopian who wanted to revolutionize family and society by creating cooperative communities.[3] Colburn, Alcott, and some others asserted that children were active thinkers rather than passive receptors, and that teaching should not consist simply of telling students what to know. They regarded childish thought as unique and valuable in its own right rather than just a beginner's version of adult cognition, and they portrayed traditional teaching as an inappropriate imposition. Children should be treated gently and with respect, as befitted those with ideas of their own, rather than in the didactic fashion that might suit the recalcitrant or empty-headed.

As the nineteenth century wore on, more educators picked up the idea that teaching should be adapted to children's understanding. John Dewey, Col. Francis Parker, and G. Stanley Hall were the

most influential; writing near the end of that century, they portrayed childhood as a distinctive stage in human development and presented children as creatures with unique interests and capacities. They argued that schools had failed students by treating them as passive receptacles rather than active learners, and they asserted that teaching should be adapted to how learners thought. This departed from earlier school-boosting doctrine in the sense that Dewey and the others asserted that learners had minds of their own and made sense of the world in their own ways, rather than having their minds made for them by society and nature. But these critics were no less attached to popular Protestant and Enlightenment ideas than the earlier reformers. They assumed that students would be utterly vulnerable to teachers once teachers understood learning and child development and adapted instruction accordingly. Dewey was by far the most sophisticated late nineteenth-century dissenter, but his faith in teachers' power to connect with learning was as unlimited as Horace Mann's, at least in his early work. He wrote that teachers who understood children's development and their unique modes of thought not only would be more effective but also would have an easier time in classrooms than traditional teachers.[4] If these American Romantics rejected a few Enlightenment and populist Protestant ideas, they improved and embellished others. Like their forebears, they saw human improvement as easy once people got the hang of it. Many educators and other reformers have kept that faith.

I propose a different view. If teachers assiduously investigate students' knowledge, they are likely to turn up a remarkable mixture of inventive ideas, insights, unfamiliar errors, and unusual formulations. The more they familiarize themselves with such things and the more they teach in response, the more opportunities they can

create to make connections with learning, the more chances they have to construct a sophisticated practice, and the more likely it is that they can devise more social resources of practice. But as teachers do such things, they encounter puzzling ideas, troubling inconsistencies, and gaps between teaching and learning. These things complicate teaching by revealing how complex and often puzzling learning is, and how fragile its connection to teaching can be.

Teachers' Orientation to Learners' Knowledge

Teachers adopt a variety of stances toward students' knowledge. Some invest little effort in exploring the connections between teaching and learning, while others explore extensively. Table 7.1 displays several of the chief alternatives. Although teachers often employ a few of these alternatives at once, they also use them separately, in

Table 7.1. Teachers' orientations to learners' knowledge

(1) Ignore what students know:	(2) Attend passively:	(3) Attend vicariously:	(4) Attend directly:
Speak but do not listen. Assume that if students listen they will learn, or that those who can learn will, and that the rest will sink. Assume that what students learn is their business.	Listen to what students say and answer some queries but take no action based on what they say. Otherwise, act as though what students learn is their business.	Read books, listen to stories, read research reports, and attend meetings. Orient teaching in response, but do not attend directly to students' knowledge or their responses to teaching.	Seek firsthand acquaintance with students' knowledge. Ask questions, listen to discussions, give exams, etc., and teach in response.

some cases because they are mutually exclusive and in some because they use them in series. Thus I consider them individually.

One of the most common stances teachers adopt is also the simplest: they ignore students' knowledge (cell 1). Many university instructors give an exam or two or assign a term paper for their courses, but they neither read the results nor seek any other information about students' grasp of course material; teaching assistants are assigned that work. Teaching of this sort can be quite self-referential; instructors present the material as they imagine it should be, not in light of knowledge about what students know, and they do not follow up by attending to what students make of instruction. Such teaching does not necessarily arise from hostility. Teachers who adopt this stance may work hard to make assignments, give lectures, and comment on course materials, but they limit teaching to those efforts. Nor is such teaching necessarily the result of indifference to students' learning. Teachers often assume equivalence between what they say and what students learn. Like eighteenth- and nineteenth-century theorists, they believe that students need only attend to teachers' words and lessons in order to learn. Or like some policy makers or executives who promulgate new policies or programs, they often leave execution to others, lower in the chain of command, to figure out for themselves. If students do not disturb such instruction, teachers can work smoothly; they judge that their instruction has been successful if they gave a good lecture. Teachers of this sort do not include students' responses in their conception of success and failure in teaching, and sometimes plow ahead even if students seem distressed or confused.

Readers may think that such work is solipsistic, but it has many analogues in everyday life. Although many people intermittently check to see whether they have been understood in common con-

versation, few do more and many do less. Checking extensively would demand much time and attention; we would regularly ask if we had been understood and often would request additional evidence. Such checks and subsidiary exchanges would chop up the flow of discourse and turn many conversations into something like research projects or cross-examinations. They also would present disturbing evidence of missed connections and misapprehensions, which could require people to retrace their steps, to try to repair the problem, and to check again. This work would tend to erode the idea that we are understood, and it would make ordinary discourse much more taxing. Most find it easier to assume that they are understood until contrary evidence is presented.

When teachers work on the unchecked assumption that they are understood, they reflect these conventional—it seems fair to term them natural—features of ordinary life. To work in this fashion is to separate teaching and learning. If teachers do not investigate what students know they are relieved of the need to confront gaps in communication and to cultivate special expertise in this area. Some chalk up students' poor performance to a failure to listen or read, or to lack of ability. Others declare an interest only in the unusual students who can work things out for themselves, and they let the rest flounder. One reason that such practices persist and even flourish is that teaching of this sort can work; learning is a distinct activity that can succeed without attentive teaching, and some students do quite well with inattentive teachers.

The remainder of Table 7.1 sketches some of the other ways in which teachers attend to learners' knowledge. Some attend passively; they listen to what students say and read what they write, but they ignore it for purposes of instruction (cell 2). Teachers pause when students comment and sometimes answer when students

question, but they do not pursue students' ideas or alter instruction in response. One familiar version of this approach is university and high-school lecturers who take questions but do not answer; they announce instead that they will "get to that later" and return to the monologue. Students participate and may learn something from one another's questions, but the questions have little impact on teaching apart from briefly interrupting it. Teachers of this sort need not cultivate special skills of inquiry into students' knowledge because they use none; ordinary interactive knowledge and skills suffice.

Another stance that teachers adopt is vicarious attention to students' knowledge (cell 3). Teachers listen to colleagues' stories, read specialized texts on learning or popular articles on student life, attend lectures on learning theory, or read studies of students' knowledge done in classes elsewhere. Acquaintance of this sort has been an important source of general enlightenment about instruction; intending primary-school teachers have learned from reading and other sources that young children are curious and easy to instruct. The informal grouping of students that one now sees in primary schools originated partly in late nineteenth-century views of child development, and some recent efforts to reform teaching rest on researchers' claims to have discovered the elements of effective instruction. Many primary-school teachers learned from reading that children think differently than adults, and they may rely on learning theory and research to inform their choices of materials to use with young children.

No teacher can avoid vicarious knowledge or using some of it in instruction, because no one can isolate herself or himself from history and social circumstances. But some teachers take no other steps to acquaint themselves with students' knowledge. They do not directly explore what students make of their words and assignments.

Instead of reading students' papers, they tell students to correct their work themselves or to correct one another's papers, or they assign such work to teaching assistants. Teachers of this sort may use secondhand accounts of students' knowledge but do not investigate what their students actually know. This sort of acquaintance with students' knowledge may include some specialized knowledge of human development, curriculum theory, or trends in adolescent taste, but it requires little special expertise.

Direct Acquaintance

In contrast, some teachers seek firsthand acquaintance with students' knowledge (cell 4). They ask questions, give tests, assign and read homework, listen to students' discussion, and more. These inquiries can open teaching to learning and make it possible to narrow the distance between them, but the ways in which teachers seek such acquaintance vary greatly. Table 7.2 sets out a few of the chief alternatives. At one extreme (cell 1) teachers' inquiries are terminal: they assess students' knowledge but do not use the results in instruction.

Table 7.2. Teachers' direct acquaintance with students' knowledge

(1) Assess learners' work but do not adjust instruction in light of the results.	(2) Probe students' knowledge, but only for congruence with teaching. Adjust instruction to improve congruence.	(3) Probe students' knowledge for signs of minds at work. Adjust instruction to improve students' understanding.

Note: This table develops category (4) in Table 7.1. Like the other tables I have presented, it deals only with categorical extremes or ideal types. Hence it represents a few sections of a continuum that contains many additional possibilities for acquaintance with students' knowledge.

Teachers' inquiries are neither intended nor designed to improve the connections between teaching and learning. In some cases this is because teachers are the instruments of others' inquiries—they give tests that are required by some external agency but are not informed in a timely way or at all about the results, or they ignore the results because they regard the exercise as irrelevant. Other teachers devise tests, assign homework, and conduct recitations only to assess learning; they do not use the results as evidence about their teaching and do not revise their teaching in light of the results. This approach assumes a tidily divided view of instruction: teachers present material, and learners study it. Students who do poorly are told to study more, harder, or better or are referred to bureaus that help with study habits and skills. In effect, teachers delegate to students or others the responsibility for dealing with the problems they uncover. Students' weak performance is taken as a sign that learners must revise their actions, not as clues that teachers should revise theirs. Teachers acquaint themselves with students' knowledge but leave teaching untouched.

Other teachers probe students' knowledge for evidence of instruction (cells 2 and 3). They read exams and homework and listen to students' comments to learn about how students think, what they know, and what they make of readings, lectures, or discussions. These teachers acquaint themselves with students' knowledge in order to improve teaching and learning; students' knowledge is important evidence about teaching, and teachers take responsibility for students' learning. No tidy division of labor between teaching and learning is assumed.

Teachers who attend to students' knowledge in this way can enrich instruction, but they complicate it. Elementary-school students commonly miss long-division problems in May that they had solved

the previous December. They invent unorthodox subtraction procedures rather than simply following the algorithms in texts or demonstrated by teachers. College and high-school students may locate the Reformation in Italy, report that Franklin D. Roosevelt was president during the Spanish-American War, or embrace Aristotelian conceptions of motion despite much instruction to the contrary. If teachers habitually ask questions in class, organize discussions or recitations, or assign and read homework, they are more likely to encounter evidence that students did not learn what had been taught than if they only attend lectures on student life and learning, read studies of effective teaching or texts on human development, or ignore students' knowledge altogether. The more first-hand evidence of students' knowledge that teachers bring to light, the more likely they are to learn that there often is no easy equivalence between teaching and learning.[5] The discrepancies provoke questions. Was their teaching off the mark, or did students simply not listen? If they did not listen, how might they be encouraged to do so? And if they did listen, would they learn more if the teaching had been different? If so, how? Would it take only more time? More discussion? More homework? More explanation? And what might be subtracted to make room for such additions? Such questions can lead teachers to connect with learners, but they can be disconcerting. Teachers depend on students for their success, and the more closely they attend to students' knowledge, the more likely it is that they will confront evidence that something is amiss, and they did not succeed.

Such problems can be troublesome, but they are not equally troublesome for everyone because teachers directly acquaint themselves with students' knowledge in very different ways. In many cases they listen only for copies of their own words and ideas (cell

2). They ask whether students got the formula right, the facts correct, or the interpretation straight and search only for evidence of fidelity of students' work to their own. The greater the fidelity, the more such teachers judge learning and teaching to be successful. This approach constrains the difficulty of acquaintance with students' knowledge because checking for congruence limits the range and complexity of what they need to notice. If students faithfully recount the ideas, facts, and operations that have been taught, teachers know that learning and teaching were on the right track, and if students deviate from those words and ideas, teachers know that things have gone awry.

Other teachers search for signs of minds at work (cell 3). They probe for evidence of what students made of instruction by attending to their inventions, mistakes, misunderstandings, and knowledge more conventionally defined.[6] Fifth-graders who are reading *Robinson Crusoe* may wonder aloud what Crusoe will think about the footprints that he discovers on the beach; their teacher may encourage them to explain their ideas, hoping to learn more about what they know of the book, how they characterize Crusoe, and how they connect these things with their knowledge of previous developments in the novel. Or, as members of a graduate U.S. Civil War history seminar discuss why the South lost, one student may assert that the lack of an industrial base was the chief culprit while another responds that it was errors of Confederate strategy. The teacher may encourage these arguments in order to learn more about what students made of the reading, how they construed authors' views, and how they use historical analysis.

When teachers search for signs of minds at work, they have a more complex task than if they check for congruence. Teachers cannot understand the sense that others are trying to make without

putting themselves into the others' mental shoes, and it is more difficult to grasp different frames of reference than to search for congruence with one's own. When teachers check for congruence, they need only ask whether the pattern of students' work matches the pattern they desire; no other inquiry is needed. But probing how learners think about the matter in question and why they think as they do is more complicated. These investigations are especially difficult when learners are only beginning to grasp the conventions that structure a field of knowledge. Students' questions, insights, and ideas may sound unfamiliar because they have imperfectly acquired the conventions to which teachers are accustomed through their success in formal education—for example, that one adds and subtracts in columns, not rows, or that one writes essays in topically delineated paragraphs, not one undifferentiated lump. To learn a field is in part to learn such conventions, but to be a learner often is to be in only partial command of them. Students' developing capabilities regularly limit their ability to explain themselves to teachers whose academic accomplishment can limit their understanding of such things. Teachers must have specialized knowledge and skills to put themselves into learners' mental shoes. They need familiarity with the subject matter in question and knowledge of the perspectives from which it has been understood; they need awareness of how learners think about the subject, skill in probing their ideas, and patient listening. This work can be rewarding because it can help improve instruction, but it is taxing, often puzzling, and sometimes distressing.

Teachers regulate those difficulties as they design different ways to probe students' knowledge. When they check only for congruence, they ease their problems by insisting that students focus on what the teacher taught, that they use familiar expressions, and the like. Such

restrictions constrain the material to which teachers must attend and the process of attending, and so limit both uncertainty about what students know and the material that teachers depend on students to produce. If teachers check for signs of minds at work, they increase their chances to make connections with learning, but only at the price of increasing uncertainty about students' knowledge and the range of work that they depend on students to produce.

Conceptions of Knowledge

Teachers cannot acquaint themselves with knowledge in general; they can explore what students know only by probing some particular construction of some particular material. If teachers view arithmetic as a system of facts and rules, they explore knowledge of those facts and rules. Teachers who take this approach want to know whether students use the correct procedures and get the right answers. They are likely to think that students do not know subtraction if they make computational errors or invent unfamiliar ways to work the problems, even if students can explain how subtraction works or why their procedure is warranted. If teachers define students' knowledge in a fairly circumscribed fashion, as command of facts and procedures, they are likely to view confusions or inventions as errors and distractions rather than signs of intelligent inquiry.[7] If, in contrast, teachers view learning arithmetic as a matter of mathematical inquiry, they work in a larger and less-well-defined terrain. They are likely to think that knowing subtraction includes knowing when the procedure is warranted and being able to explain why. They want to know whether students can work problems and get the right answers, but also whether students can explain and justify their work. They are likely to view approximations of

good answers, errors, and inventions as useful evidence of what students know.

What some teachers see as important ideas, clues to learning, and evidence of thoughtfulness, others see as errors, distractions, or irrelevancies. Treating learners' work as right and wrong answers or correct and incorrect procedures can restrict teachers' difficulty in learning about learning by simplifying what students produce and what teachers need to comprehend; in contrast, treating students' work as evidence of their learning mathematical inquiry complicates what students produce, what teachers need to comprehend, and teachers efforts' to probe learning.

Some readers may think that these last few paragraphs are misguided. If teachers view learning as the acquisition of a practice of inquiry, does it not follow that they would never check for evidence on the congruence between students' thinking and their own? Would teachers who saw knowledge as fixed ever investigate students' thinking? Is not a view of knowledge by definition also a view of how to acquaint oneself with students' knowledge?

Perhaps it would be if teachers were utterly consistent. But in practice some teachers who view knowledge as fixed nonetheless carefully probe what students make of instruction, and others who believe that learning is the acquisition of a practice check students' work for congruence with their own ideas. The processes through which teachers acquaint themselves with students' knowledge are at least partly independent of how they view and extend knowledge; teachers who hold similar views of knowledge often employ very different approaches to learning about students' learning.

Table 7.3 displays some of the chief alternatives. Most common are teachers who view knowledge as fixed and search students' knowledge for congruence with their own (cell 1). Teachers who take this

Table 7.3. Conceptions of knowledge and modes of acquaintance with students' knowledge

Modes of acquaintance with students' knowledge	Conceptions of knowledge	
	Fixed	Practice of inquiry
Check for congruence	(1) Teachers may be closely acquainted with surface strata of students' knowledge by systematic checks of students' grasp of facts and rules. Deep familiarity with students' ideas, misunderstandings, and the like is unlikely.	(2) Teachers may be closely acquainted with students' capacity to reproduce relatively complex knowledge, but they usually lack deep acquaintance with students' ideas, misunderstandings, and the like.
Attend to signs of minds at work	(3) Teachers may be closely acquainted with students' knowledge and more familiar than in (1) with what students make of instruction, but the depth and extent of their familiarity usually are limited.	(4) Teachers have extensive acquaintance with students' ideas, inventions, misunderstandings, and the like.

approach can become quite familiar with certain strata of students' knowledge; they can discern which problems students are able to solve and what mistakes are most common and can focus instruction accordingly. Such acquaintance has been central to conceptions of instruction that stress "basic skills" and "effective" teaching. Teachers who work in these ways try to present knowledge in a clear and orderly fashion, check for students' acquisition of that knowledge, and use the results of such checks to inform the next instructional steps.[8]

Teaching in this way also differs depending on the discourse organization that teachers use. Table 7.4 summarizes several alternatives. Many teachers (cell 1) rely mainly on indirect interaction to explore what students know—written homework, multiple-choice tests, fill-in-the-blank exercises, workbook problems, seatwork, and checklists. Students' responses can be checked against a text or an answer sheet, or graded by a teaching assistant or tabulated by a publisher or an evaluation contractor. These measures leave teachers little room to probe students' knowledge in depth, and students have few opportunities to probe back, whether in distance learning or classrooms dominated by seatwork. The demands on teachers' knowledge and skill are constrained because inquiries and responses are kept on the surface of knowledge, and modest interactive skill is required.

In contrast, many teachers use direct interaction to probe students' knowledge (cell 2). They schedule regular recitations, question students about material, read homework, and find other ways to acquaint themselves with what students know. Such direct probing gives teachers somewhat more room to investigate students' knowledge, and it gives students a bit more room to probe back. This requires more interactive skill, but the demands on teachers' knowledge of the material are not great because teachers have few opportunities to explore students' knowledge progressively. Because teachers probe students' knowledge in discrete bits rather than deepening inquiry, they need to know those bits and to connect them only as lists on a page, headings under a topic, or parts of an assignment. Though some teachers who work in this way know the material deeply they need not, nor do they require many special skills of probing students' knowledge. Because the appeal of this approach is not tightly tied to teachers' knowledge—well informed university and high-school teachers use it—improving teachers'

Table 7.4. How interactions among discourse organization, views of knowledge, and acquaintance with students' knowledge bear on teaching

	Explore in indirect interaction	Explore in direct interaction
View knowledge as fixed and search for congruence	(1) Use multiple-choice tests, homework or seatwork handouts, checklists, and similar devices to probe students' knowledge. Teachers and students cannot explore in depth because of constraints in the view of knowledge, the mode of exploration, and the discourse. Students' probing of teachers' views is quite limited. Teachers require little interactive skill and little knowledge of exploratory techniques. Prepackaged assessments are typical.	(2) Use simple question and answer or formal recitations to probe students' knowledge. The depth and extent of exploration are limited because of constraints in the view of knowledge and the mode of exploration. Although the discourse format also restricts probing, it is less restrictive than indirect interactions. Students can probe teachers' knowledge in return, but usually not extensively. Teachers need some interactive skill and knowledge and some capacity to frame appropriate questions and quickly assess answers.
View knowledge as the outcome of inquiry, and search for signs of minds at work	(3) Use essays, journal writing, and the like to explore what students know and how well they can explain it. Students and teachers can explore in considerable depth. Teachers may encourage students to probe teachers' knowledge in return. Teachers require little interactive skill and knowledge, but they need considerable specialized knowledge of the subject to ask good questions and respond thoughtfully to students' answers.	(4) Use discussions, debates, extended colloquies, and other direct discourses to probe what students know. Students may be encouraged to challenge one another's knowledge and even that of the teacher. Teachers require considerable knowledge of the material, interactive skill, and ways to combine the two.

knowledge of a subject may not alter the teaching. For such teaching limits uncertainty about what students know, be it elementary subtraction or advanced statistics, and the conception of knowledge and the method of exploring it constrain other sources of ambiguity: answers must be selected from those given, only one answer may be chosen, only the blanks may be filled in, and answers are right or wrong. Reports of this sort are clear, crisp, and relatively easy to grasp; it is relatively easy to tell when students have succeeded or failed. Truth and error seem plain, and instruction is relatively easy to manage. This approach also constrains teachers' dependence on students by limiting both the complexity of students' responses to teachers' probes and the performances that teachers depend on students to produce. Students also may encourage teachers to work in this way, either because they are habituated to it or because they have little tolerance for uncertainty. Acquaintance with students' knowledge is one medium in which teachers and students regulate their relations, and teachers who use these approaches can practice attentively while constraining difficulty.

At the other extreme, some teachers view knowledge as evidence of learners' work as novice inquirers in a field and seek close acquaintance with their thinking (Table 7.4, cells 3 and 4). They encourage students to make reasonable estimates, to invent solutions to difficult problems, to explore their errors, and to explain why they attacked a problem in one way rather than another. Such work can be quite productive because the more effectively teachers elicit students' ideas and the more deeply they are acquainted with students' knowledge, the more intelligently they can design instruction in response. But students' efforts to make sense of material often lead them into puzzles, disagreements, and ideas that are partly understood or murkily expressed. The more teachers invite students to serve up

such material, the more complexity they have to deal with. It can be quite demanding to attend carefully to one student's ideas, and more demanding to attend to the ideas of twenty. If we add thoughtful response to this approach, the work is even more difficult.

Some teachers ease these demands by using indirect interaction to explore what sense students make of instruction (Table 7.4, cell 3). University faculty members assign essays or ask students to write journals to acquaint themselves with students' written efforts to make sense of instruction. If they make thoughtful assignments and read intelligently, they can learn about students' ideas without discussion or debate. Such work takes considerable knowledge and intellectual skill, but because teachers probe students' knowledge by reading papers in their offices, they need no interactive knowledge or skill. They can deal with uncertainty and dependence in the privacy of their minds, not the public arena of a class.

The demands are much greater if teachers probe students' efforts to make sense of instruction in discussion or other direct discourse (Table 7.4, cell 4). They must try to figure out whether students are making sense of one another's ideas while helping them make such sense, attempting to figure out what students mean, and managing their work together. Instead of crisp, right or wrong answers, teachers focus on ideas, arguments, and other evidence of efforts to understand. To do such work, teachers must open windows on learners' knowledge, but when they do, all sorts of things may fly in. Teachers cannot do such work well unless they have deep knowledge of the material and how learners think about it, and can manage complex social interactions concerning these matters. They must be able to deal with considerable uncertainty in the class because probing students' knowledge in this way is likely to elicit conflicting ideas and ambiguity. Teachers also must be able to cope with extensive and

visible dependence on learners, since the work will not go well unless students offer useful evidence and ideas; if they are silent or offer entirely off-the-wall comments, teachers can seem to fail in the public arena of the class.

It takes both generosity of spirit and the capacity to put oneself in learners' intellectual places for teachers to consistently try to see things from learners' perspectives. Yet teaching and learning will not go well unless teachers also have a clear sense of quality work. They must cultivate a sort of dual consciousness: on the one hand intellectual selflessness as they seek to learn what sense students make of material and use that learning to inform teaching, but on the other deep knowledge of the material and a clear view of the nature of good work.[9] Teachers can learn to work in this way but it has been unnatural, contrary to both conventional teaching and to the habits of ordinary conversation.

Work of this sort is not easy anywhere, but it has been especially difficult in the United States. The absence of a common curriculum has meant that teachers have not developed common knowledge about how students respond to particular assignments, what their likely misunderstandings are, and how they might usefully respond to students' work. The absence of this knowledge has meant that teacher education cannot be oriented to these matters, so most intending teachers have entered classrooms quite unprepared either to investigate students' understanding or to respond to their ideas. The lack of other traditions of practice, such as lesson study, in which teachers work together to improve lessons by identifying what students make of the material, has left practicing teachers without the social resources that a developed professional community that was focused on improving instruction could offer. Absent these things, teachers who have sought to deeply acquaint themselves with stu-

dents' knowledge have had to use their own resources in isolation. It is no surprise that most teachers have taken less demanding paths.

Most of the time, most of us act as though we are understood. Although we intermittently check on whether we are understood, we usually accept the polite assurances that come without asking for much supporting evidence. Only occasionally do we press our conversational partners to explain what they make of our words; when we do, we are often surprised by how their understanding differs from our own. Despite such surprises, we usually plow ahead, acting as though we embraced beliefs that were just upset. The assumptions that we are understood and that understanding is one mind's copy of another seem to be two of the tougher threads in the fabric of everyday life.

Teachers embrace the same beliefs and face the same puzzles, but they carry some additional baggage. Because their task is to help students understand, students' grasp of teachers' words and assignments carries particular weight, for students are less likely to succeed if mutual understanding among them, and between them and teachers, is weak. Ordinary discourse is rarely freighted with that responsibility. Hence one of the more constructive things a teacher can do is to acquaint herself with students' knowledge and adapt instruction accordingly. But teachers are not just instruments for someone else's improvement; they also seek success and depend on students for it. How their words and assignments are understood counts heavily. To turn up evidence that students have not learned is one of the most threatening things teachers can do; a student who fails to comprehend is an actual or potential failure for the teacher. The more vivid the evidence that students did not learn, the more troublesome it can be.

This is another predicament of teaching: acquaintance with students' knowledge is full of promise but loaded with problems. Every teacher adopts some stance toward this acquaintance, deliberately or not, and I have interpreted those stances in part as ways to manage the predicament. At one extreme, teachers insulate themselves from acquaintance with students' knowledge or very sharply limit it. They close off opportunities to learn about students' learning and chances to improve it, and so protect themselves against knowledge of failure.

A few alternatives enable teachers to manage the predicament more attentively but cautiously. They can closely monitor certain strata of students' knowledge, search for signs of correct and incorrect performance, give clear signals about what work is acceptable, and adjust teaching in response to these elements of students' work. Teachers seek evidence of students' learning, but because they construe knowledge as fixed or monitor only for congruence with their own ideas, they narrow the range of successes and problems that they turn up. This approach makes it relatively easy to identify problems and take steps to repair them. When teaching of this sort turns up evidence of learning problems, teachers can respond in ways that create opportunities to improve students' performance and make learning a better copy of teaching. That narrows what is meant by understanding, but it also narrows the problems with which teachers must deal.

But when teachers construe knowledge as the result of efforts to make sense of material and probe for signs of minds at work, they confront the predicament more fully. If they teach in ways that increase students' opportunities to make sense of instruction and deeply acquaint themselves with students' knowledge, teachers increase the chances that students' inventions, confusions, and arguments will become part of the class's work. That increases teachers'

opportunities to learn what students know and how they think and to revise instruction in ways that may improve students' understanding. But they cannot do so without inviting evidence that students did not learn, are confused, or learned something else than was intended, all of which can be taken as evidence that teachers may not have succeeded.

Teachers who work in this way must suspend the usual view that they are understood in favor of the unnatural idea that understanding must be attentively checked and double-checked. They must suspend the common belief that learning is a copy of teaching in favor of the view that learning is sense making of different sorts, and that learners' ideas deserve to be respectfully heard, investigated, and accepted, if they can be rationally presented and defended. Teachers must know a great deal and be skillful inquirers into others' knowledge in order to do such work, but they also must make themselves vulnerable to evidence of failure that most of us regularly avoid. Work of this sort is difficult in any circumstances, but it is especially difficult in the United States, where public education offers few of the social resources that can make it less taxing for teachers to connect learning with teaching.

8

IMPROVE TEACHING

One reason that I did the research for this book was to improve my understanding, and I hope that of others, of teaching and its sister occupations. Another was to figure out why teaching practice—work with students that is intellectually demanding, attentive to students' work, and conducive to thoughtful conversation—has been so difficult to achieve and sustain in the United States. If I could do these two things, I might be able to shed some light on two other questions: what would it take to make teaching practice more available, and why have many recent reforms been disappointing? I pull together the key elements of my analysis of the first two matters, which were spread across the preceding chapters, to probe the last two.

The key point in my analysis has been that U.S. public education is not organized to help teachers manage the predicaments of their occupation in ways that support work with students that is intellectually demanding, attentive to students' work, and conducive to thoughtful conversation. Like psychotherapists, social workers, and workers in some other occupations, teachers aim to improve our thoughts, feelings, beliefs, organizations, and knowledge. Several predicaments are endemic in such work. Although human improvers

typically are more educated and qualified than their younger, weaker, or damaged clients, they depend on their clients' success for their own success. Because they cannot work at all without clients' engagement and cannot do ambitious work without clients' active and intelligent engagement, human improvers depend on their clients' will and capability to improve.

In addition, no matter how refined improvers' expertise is, it is regularly inadequate. One reason is uncertainty about the ends and means of practice; another is the unpredictability of work with other humans. Practitioners thus require supplements to expertise, most notably hope, courage, and persistence. These are not features of expertise, but without them, expertise cannot flourish. Indeed, the more ambitious the work the more uncertainties and surprises turn up, for which there often are no familiar or professionally accepted solutions; these uncertainties and surprises require even more supplements. Expertise is precious but chronically insufficient.

Why has public education not helped teachers manage these predicaments in ways that support teaching practice?

My answer began with the design of government. Jeffersonian distrust of government ("that government is best which governs least") and economic liberalism led states to do little to develop capability to manage or improve instruction. Most states instead outsourced the core elements of infrastructure, most prominently curriculum and tests, to private firms. Other features of government's design—federalism, the separation of powers, and local control—made coherent action quite difficult within states and localities and even within schools. These features impeded development of educational infrastructure: the schools have had no common curricula or curriculum frameworks, no common exams that were tied

to the curricula, no common practices that were grounded in the curricula, and no teacher education that focused on teaching the curricula that students would study.

The mere presence of these things would not assure quality education; that would depend on how infrastructure was designed and how educators used it, and use would depend on the capability of school systems, the people who work in them, and how society supported their work. But because teachers in the United States have lacked these resources, they have had great difficulty building shared occupational knowledge and skills. They have had no common framework with which to make valid judgments about students' work and no common vocabulary with which to identify, investigate, discuss, and solve problems of teaching and learning. Hence they also have had little common knowledge that could be systematized for use in the education of intending teachers. Individual teachers developed knowledge and skills, and some became quite expert, but public education has had no developed means to turn teachers' individual knowledge and skill into common know-how, let alone to remember it, improve it by analysis, and make it available to novices. Weak social resources have impoverished the occupation and impeded the development of individual teachers' knowledge and skill.

The political fragmentation of school governance and the lack of means to build common knowledge of teaching also meant that when teachers organized, they did so chiefly around pressing bread-and-butter issues of wages, working conditions, and civil liberties, not educational issues. It often is said that firms get the unions they deserve and teacher unions historically reflected local school districts' inattention to building knowledge and skills for improved practice; for most of their history, the American Federation of

Teachers and the National Education Association did not put building the knowledge and skills of teaching high on their list of issues for collective bargaining and so did not contribute to building a knowledgeable occupation.

The design of governance also meant that schools were for the most part locally financed, and growing economic and racial segregation led to an increasingly unequal distribution of educational resources among districts within states and among schools in many districts. That inequality combined with students' very unequal social and economic backgrounds to make it very difficult to offer quality education in the poorest schools. Fiscal inequality within states has been very difficult to remedy because most schemes to equalize resources among districts run head-on into the political structure of local government. As states have taken a larger role in school finance, differences in wealth among states have been reflected in large inequality among states in expenditures on schools.

Local control and the separation of powers also made school governance very permeable and created many openings for pressure groups to urge their views. A design of government that opened access to contending interests and ideologies also created disincentives for teaching that might provoke conflict. The growth of public education into a compulsory, mass-attended, batch-processing enterprise also meant that few public schools or school systems organized to build mutual commitment to improvement.

U.S. schools thus combine very loose organization and little common knowledge of teaching; there have been few formal constraints on how teachers teach, but few opportunities to develop traditions of ambitious practice. For most of U.S. history, teachers could teach as they preferred with little interference, fashioning their responses to texts, reforms, and other advice as long as their work provoked

no conflict with parents and students did not get out of hand. Because teacher education has typically been weak, the strongest influences on how most teachers learned to teach were their experiences as students in K–12 classrooms and their initial exposure to classroom work as beginning teachers. Most teaching in the United States thus has been quite conventional since the outset of public education. Moreover, such teaching was passed across generations of teachers, with little interference from clear and coherent guidance for instruction, or from sustained help to improve teaching.

Ambitious teaching is difficult in any circumstances, but it is especially difficult if schools lack the common knowledge, organization, and occupational culture that can support it. Teaching in the mainstream has as a result generally been weak, and teaching practice has been more likely in enclaves like the Advanced Placement Program that offer some social resources to support it.

It is often said that teachers inflexibly resist change; reformers view teaching as an occupation of glacial disposition. Some teachers certainly are inflexible, but in several years of observing responses to state and federal reforms, I found that most teachers tried to respond constructively. But they did so in the only ways they could—in light of their knowledge and experience, the sense they could make of the often vague advice that came their way, and the very little assistance that they were offered. The suppleness of teaching, the lack of infrastructure, and loose organization left them room to frame their responses but constrained the depth of those responses. Teachers made what they saw as major changes, but reformers and observers saw them as quite limited.[1]

Substantial improvement in teaching will depend on finding ways to overcome the conditions sketched here, especially the lack of coherent infrastructure, means to make good use of it, and means to

mobilize mutual commitment to improvement. Most recent reform efforts—performance pay, school turnaround, and accountability—do not address these matters and take an unfortunately narrow and instrumental view of teaching. They treat teaching almost entirely as an agent for the improvement of learning and frame the task as though it is a matter of weak individuals, when the weakness is systemic.

School turnaround, for example, is a central feature of recent federal and state policies, but although many schools enter restructuring, few exit successfully, even after many years. When schools do make significant changes, they are difficult to sustain. Studies of school turnaround agree that the work is very difficult and that success is rare, with a success rate of 20 or 25 percent.[2] Accounts of heroic and apparently successful efforts to turn weak schools into strong ones are few and far between.[3] The Center on Education Policy studied such efforts in five states; its report on California concluded that "federal restructuring strategies have very rarely helped schools improve student achievement."[4]

Two features of the turnaround strategy help explain these results. One is that it has not attended to educational content. Turnaround success is said to depend on strong new leadership, dismissal of teachers and hiring new staff, the use of "distinguished educators" to advise principals and teachers, and tight student discipline that includes dismissing students who reject the regime. Curriculum, teaching, and teacher education have rarely been mentioned.[5] The other is that each school to be turned around is treated as an individual failure that must be repaired individually. These schools' problems are not seen as evidence of system failure, and turnaround efforts do not treat them as part of educational systems. But if each school must be turned around on its own,

apart from a common instructional frame, success requires reinvention of the educational wheel in each school. Maintaining success would require continuing heroic efforts to sustain each school, absent assistance from a system that is designed to support improvement. When school improvement is understood and dealt with in this individualistic manner, the barriers to success increase because the capability to offer quality education is more difficult to build and sustain in stand-alone schools.

Performance pay is another feature of the current reforms. The aim is to distinguish more qualified individual teachers by using longitudinal measures of student achievement—value-added measures of student performance—to estimate each teacher's contribution to students' learning. The aim is to reward teachers whose students gain more, or eliminate those teachers whose students gain less, or both. Performance pay promises large improvement in student performance without a huge investment in system redesign. The idea has wide appeal: President Obama and Education Secretary Duncan favor performance pay, as do some governors, state legislators, business critics of public education, and several large foundations. In response to federal and foundation incentives, several states and localities are trying to devise and implement such schemes.

One problem with performance pay is that the United States lacks an instructional system that would enable valid determinations of which teachers boost students' test scores. Another is that researchers report that performance pay does not boost students' scores, and still another is that existing tests do not support defensible determinations of teaching quality, except perhaps at the very extremes of the distribution.[6] One reason for the last point is that the tests have limited reliability—scores on one administration of a test weakly predict scores on another administration of the same

test a week or two later.[7] Tests also do not agree very well; different parts of the same tests that attempt to measure the same academic content yield different results.[8] Moreover, students who take such tests and their teachers do not have equal access to educational resources, and some teachers systematically get more able or less able students.[9] For these reasons and several others, the existing tests can incorrectly identify teachers as effective or not.[10]

A coherent infrastructure in the United States could enable valid judgments about the quality of teaching and learning and about which teachers do a better job of helping students learn. If teachers and students used a common curriculum, they could have less unequal chances to teach and learn. There could be assessments of students' learning that were valid for the common curriculum, so students and teachers could have less unequal chances to be tested on what they were supposed to have taught and learned. Teachers also could have opportunities to learn how to teach the common curriculum in preservice or later professional education.

Accountability policies—the third key reform—aim to improve teaching by making school staffs responsible for students' performance. If students do well on tests, school staffs may be rewarded, but if they do not, school staffs either must correct the situation or face job loss, new leadership, or retraining. These policies assume that the causes of weak student learning lie chiefly in teachers' deficient sense of responsibility, determination, and hard work. Some teachers are not responsible or determined, but dealing with that small fraction of the teaching force would not remedy the chief causes of weak student performance—teachers' weak knowledge and skills, and the infrastructure to support them. That weakness is especially pronounced in the high-poverty schools at which accountability has been chiefly aimed, and for that reason account-

ability policies have set off a chain of disappointing events. Lacking the capability to seriously improve teaching and learning, many states defined excellence down by adopting weak academic standards and/or setting the passing points on tests low. That restricted the number of failing schools, but it also seriously weakened the reforms. Thus Mississippi, which is one of the poorest states and has one of the weakest school systems, reported that a bit less than 10 percent of students were not "proficient," while Massachusetts, which is one of the most prosperous states and has one of the strongest school systems, reported that nearly half of its students were not proficient.[11] Mississippi adopted some of the least demanding tests and standards, while Massachusetts adopted some of the most demanding tests and standards. The tests often have become a protocurriculum as teachers in many schools drilled students to prepare them for the tests, an approach that is far from the academically demanding instruction that the policies proposed. There also has been evidence of teachers doctoring test results or removing students from testing if they were likely to depress scores. Like the other two policy approaches just discussed, accountability aims to improve instruction without direct work on instruction.

These three reforms have had several constructive effects. They helped call attention to America's longest-running educational problems, they stimulated private and public work on the problems, and they drew attention to inequality in public education. But the reforms have two key weaknesses: they do not build the social resources that could support quality instruction, and they treat teachers purely as agents for the improvement of learning. But my analysis implies that teachers' agency—their actions, dispositions, and expertise—must be useful in two very different ways if it is to be useful at all. Teachers' actions can be the means to improve students'

learning, but they also are means by which teachers solve problems that arise as they try to improve students' learning. Ambitious teaching boosts the chances of impressive learning, but only by increasing the difficulty of the work, the uncertainty with which teachers must cope, their vulnerability to students' performance, and the risk of failure. If teachers constrain their ambitions for students and deploy less sophisticated skills and knowledge, they limit the chances of dramatic improvement for students, but they also limit the risks and difficulty of their work. If the social resources that could support ambitious teaching are absent, the costs to teachers of ambitious teaching rise dramatically, and the likelihood of sustained good work falls.

Those social resources have long been thin, but for the first time there are promising efforts to create them. There are, for example, new educational systems that mobilize mutual commitment to improvement, build educational infrastructure, and develop capability for further growth. They include America's Choice, Core Knowledge, and Success for All, three comprehensive school reform designs (CSRDs) that have significantly improved teaching and learning in several thousand high-poverty elementary schools.[12] These designs devised extensive and often quite detailed designs for teaching and learning. They recruited and educated staff to help faculty in high-poverty schools learn to use the designs effectively. They offered extensive and continuing support for schools' use of the designs, including education for teachers and school managers that was tied to the instructional designs. They monitored educational quality in schools and took corrective action when problems arose. They linked schools in networks that supported the schools' work and encouraged the growth of communities of practice, and they created hub organizations that sponsored and supported these elements of edu-

cational infrastructure. Several charter networks, including Aspire, Achievement First, and Uncommon Schools, appear to do similar work, though on a smaller scale and with schools that the charter agencies sponsor and operate.

From one perspective these initiatives seem modest because they deal with a small number of the many weak schools that need assistance, but from another they are quite impressive because they are creating and using the social resources that are needed to build school systems that can sustain ambitious teaching and learning. But one thing that neither the CSRDs nor the charter networks can do is to cultivate common knowledge of ambitious teaching and learning that crosses the networks' boundaries. Accomplishing that would require the sort of common infrastructure that has long been absent in public education. The Common Core Initiative (CCI) could become that framework. State education chiefs and governors sponsor the CCI, nearly all the states have adopted the new standards, and most comments suggest that they are a substantial improvement on most state standards.

This is an impressive accomplishment in the fragmented landscape of U.S. education, but those standards are only a first step in what would be a long march to coherent and usable infrastructure. In their first publication, governors and state education chiefs recognized that; they write that once standards were written and adopted, states would have to take several other giant steps if the standards were to be realized in practice:

> Leverage states' collective influence to ensure that textbooks, digital media, curricula, and assessments are aligned to internationally benchmarked standards and draw on lessons from high-performing nations and states . . .

Revise state policies for recruiting, preparing, developing, and supporting teachers and school leaders to reflect the human capital practices of top-performing nations and states around the world . . .

Hold schools and systems accountable through monitoring, interventions, and support to ensure consistently high performance, drawing upon international best practices . . .

Measure state-level education performance globally by examining student achievement and attainment in an international context to ensure that, over time, students are receiving the education they need to compete.[13]

These few sentences sketch an extraordinary agenda for change, nothing less than the development of new systems of curriculum, educational media, professional education, assessment, management, and quality control—the key elements of educational infrastructure. Compared with these steps, writing standards is easy.

One reason that implementing these giant steps will be difficult is that state and local school systems will have to be much more explicit about what will be taught and learned, if the Common Core is to work. Most schools, school systems, and governments have long avoided such explicitness because clarity often led to conflict. Leaders of the Common Core say that standards will be leaner, more coherent, and more rigorous, but Americans today disagree deeply about what should be taught and learned, as they have done since the beginning of public education. One way to avoid conflict has been to paper over disagreements with vague language that offers little specific guidance, something which many standards did in the past. Another way, familiar from many standards and textbooks, is to include nearly everything, but this also offers little guidance.

Can standards be rigorous, coherent, and lean and still avoid debilitating conflict about what should be taught? The mission is not impossible, but Michael J. Petrilli, vice president of the Thomas B. Fordham Institution and an advocate of high standards, has said, "All the groups, the math educators and the English professors and the liberals and the conservatives will want to weigh in . . . There are fundamental disagreements in our society about what kids should learn."[14] Many of the points at issue are old; some date to the origins of public education. Americans have little experience with setting such differences aside in order to advance a larger, common educational interest; we have a political system that offers many openings for influence; and we are more deeply divided than at any time in living memory. These factors do not promise an easy path for implementation of the Common Core.

As I write, in the winter of 2011, it is impossible not to consider what members of the Tea Party movement will make of state plans to implement common standards for teaching and learning in local schools. It would be surprising if many state and local school systems did not face intense opposition from this political movement, as well as from groups across the political spectrum; there could be opposing slates for school board elections and threats to abandon public schools for charters or home schools. These are not problems that state or local school leaders relish, especially when revenues are falling and opposition to higher taxes is intense.

Another problem that is likely to arise as states move to implement the new standards is "alignment": are curricula consistent with the standards, are assessments consistent with the standards and curricula, and so on? This problem arises in part from unfamiliarity because consistency among the elements of education has so rarely been sought in the United States that we have little experience

in trying to observe and measure it. It also arises in part because valid judgments about consistency are difficult to make. There are, for example, several quite different ways to teach arithmetic, some traditional and didactic, others less conventional, and still others tied to particular conceptions of mathematical content. Mathematicians and mathematics educators often disagree intensely about such matters, and it would be surprising if such disputes did not erupt if states do try to achieve alignment. The American default in matters of this sort, again, has been either vague language that tries to paper over deep differences or to include nearly everything. The problem is sufficiently daunting that it has prompted Jack Jennings, an astute observer of education policy, to suggest that an independent agency might be better able than states to make the relevant determinations.[15] This idea is appealing because, among other things, economies of scale could reduce the cost of studying alignment. But would states hand over such decisions when governors and legislators are accountable for the results? Would publishers support them? Are there organizations that have the knowledge to reach valid decisions about alignment? No one knows the precise answers, but they would not be strongly affirmative.

Why not? To solve the alignment problem would include getting publishers of the textbooks, digital media, and curricula that the Common Core authors mentioned to align them with standards and assessments (which remain to be created). Would states be able to make test and text publishers align their products to CCI standards? Private firms do most publishing, and publishing of textbooks and tests is dominated by a handful of large firms, so it would be no small feat to persuade them to seriously redo their products to fit with the clear and lean CCI standards. The more states' enactment of the standards varied, the more difficult it

would be to persuade publishers to align their products. The state officials' original report envisioned groups of states combining to use joint purchasing power to get what they want, but to do that effectively, groups of states would have to have the market muscle to persuade publishers and the capability to be clear about what they wanted and to judge whether they got it. State education agencies have never invested much in making decisions about content coverage, their staffs have little expertise in such matters, and many state budgets are deep in deficit, and sinking.

There are several other fundamental problems. Can states mobilize the capability to give clear and strong guidance to teaching and teacher education? Can states mobilize the capability to help schools and teacher educators offer more focused and coherent instruction? These things would require agreement not only on standards—that is the relatively easy part—but also on the content and quality of instruction and teacher education. Those are realms in which few states or university teacher education programs have much capability.

Even if we assume that the answers to these questions are all positive, one other problem remains: the existence of standards, curriculum, and assessments is not equivalent to use, let alone effective use. In 2010 Larry Shumway, the Utah state school superintendent, told state school board members from western states that common standards are "an opportunity to do the right thing." But much remains before "educators figure out how to teach all students to those standards. I hope you'll come away from this meeting with a knot in the pit of your stomach about how far we have to go . . . It should keep you up at night."[16] One challenge that would remain, for example, would be creating extensive opportunities for teachers, school leaders, and teacher educators to learn how to do

things that few of them now know how to do. Here again, few education organizations have the capability to enable such learning.

Though the tasks would be very challenging, for the first time in U.S. history we can see how the work could be begun, and we can see organizations that could help. The charter networks and CSRDs that I discussed earlier contain the sorts of social resources that could help schools to use the curricula that might be created, following on the Common Core. But doing that work on a larger scale will require states to support organizations like these that have a proven record of effectiveness and could undertake to build or help to build additional networks of schools. Those organizations have the human resources and educational instruments to begin such work; with state and federal assistance they could begin to develop the means to replicate themselves in state or regional networks.

In 2010–2011 New York State invited independent, nonuniversity organizations to offer teacher education on the view that improvement there is badly needed, and at least one program was authorized in 2011. Given the problems of teacher supply and the weakness of university teacher education, other states could follow suit by enabling CSRDs and charter networks that have solid records of improved instruction to educate intending teachers—something they do in any event for their own recruits—as an integral part of their operations.

Although these developments are evidence of progress, a great deal remains to be done. Success of the Common Core will require much more capable state agencies, much less local control, and perhaps the creation of regional systems within or among states. Unfortunately, such major changes in government and education are quite difficult now in the age of the Tea Party and fiscal crisis. Wholesale and rapid change in the occupation of teaching also is unlikely. Salaries are not

likely to rise to levels that would attract many much more able applicants to careers in teaching. Improvement in the design of teaching that would help recruit and retain more able teachers—more work in instructional teams, less face time with students, and more opportunities for leadership within teaching—also are likely to be difficult in the current political and fiscal circumstances.

Significant improvement in teaching is more likely to be a long march than the quick fix that most recent reforms envision. But this sketch of the difficulties that face efforts to improve teaching is not an argument against such improvement—it is badly needed. Education should be much more lively, thoughtful, and humane. Understanding what that kind of education will require from schools, government, and society can only help.

Notes

2. HUMAN IMPROVEMENT

1. See, for example, *Report of the National Reading Panel: Teaching Children to Read; An Evidence-Based Assessment of the Scientific Research Literature on Reading and Its Implications for Reading Instruction* (Washington, DC: National Institute of Child Health and Human Development, 2000), and compare it with E. D. Hirsch, *The Knowledge Deficit* (Boston: Houghton Mifflin, 2006), chaps. 2, 3, and 4.

2. There are several sources for the following discussion of uncertainty. One is the historical literature on the rise of education and other social services, which traces expanding aspirations and arguments; see, for example, Lawrence Cremin, *The Transformation of the School: Progressivism in American Education, 1876–1957* (New York: Harper and Row, 1968). Another is philosophical discourse about epistemology, especially in the philosophy of science; see Stephen Toulmin, *Human Understanding* (Princeton, NJ: Princeton University Press, 1972). Still another is argument about the nature of social science knowledge; see David Braybroke and Charles E. Lindblom, *A Strategy of Decision* (New York: Free Press, 1963), and Charles E. Lindblom, *Inquiry and Change* (New Haven, CT: Yale University Press, 1990).

3. Throughout I use the term "practitioner" as a synonym of "worker" only to reduce repetition, not to signify some elevated skill or knowledge.

4. See R. D. Laing, *The Divided Self: A Study of Sanity and Madness* (Chicago: Quadrangle Books, 1960); and Thomas Szasz, *The Myth of Psychotherapy: Mental Healing as Religion, Rhetoric, and Repression* (Garden City, NY: Anchor-Doubleday, 1978).

5. See Paul Goodman, *Compulsory Mis-education and the Community of Scholars* (New York: Vintage, 1964); Edgar Friedenberg, *Coming of Age in America* (New York: Random House, 1965); and Samuel Bowles and Herbert Gintis, *Schooling in Capitalist America* (New York: Basic Books, 1976).

6. Willard Waller made this point central to his analysis in *The Sociology of Teaching*, first published in 1932 (New York: J. Wiley, 1965). Charles Bidwell offered a more formal account a few decades later in "The School as a Formal Organization," in *Handbook of Organizations*, ed. J. G. March, 973-1023 (Chicago: Rand McNally and Company, 1965). In his classic book *Schoolteacher: A Sociological Study* (Chicago: University of Chicago Press, 1975), Dan Lortie connected many of these ideas about school organization to classroom practice.

7. Commentators on teaching have long noticed the importance of resistance to teaching. See, for example, chapter 5 in Edward Eggleston, *The Hoosier Schoolmaster* (1871), an account of teaching in rural America, first published as a magazine serial; for a current, easily available version, see http://www.schooltales.net/hoosier schoolmaster. Resistance is everywhere in Waller's *Sociology of Teaching*; for a good example, see p. 445 ff.

8. Arthur Powell, Eleanor Farrar, and David K. Cohen discuss such negotiation in *The Shopping Mall High School* (Boston: Houghton Mifflin, 1985).

9. There is occasional recognition of difficulty and risk in educational commentary, but they have not been seen as central problems. However, difficulty and risk have been viewed as central in

psychotherapy. Such differences in theories about work help set expectations for what practitioners can accomplish.

10. Ann Berlak and Harold Berlak, *Dilemmas of Schooling: Teaching and Social Change* (London: Methuen, 1981); Magdalene Lampert, "How Do Teachers Manage to Teach?" *Harvard Educational Review* 55, no. 2 (2001): 178-194.

11. Most recently, see Sarah Blaffer Hrdy, *Mothers and Others: The Evolutionary Origins of Mutual Understanding* (Cambridge, MA: Harvard University Press, 2009), 1-64.

12. I take this term from Janet Malcolm, *Psychoanalysis: The Impossible Profession* (New York: Vintage, 1981), and Shoshana Felman's discussion of Freud and Lacan, "Psychoanalysis and Education: Teaching Terminable and Interminable," *Yale French Studies*, no. 63 (1982): 21-44.

13. On teachers' management of dilemmas, see Magdalene Lampert, *Teaching Problems and the Problems of Teaching* (New Haven, CT: Yale University Press, 2001); and Berlak and Berlak, *Dilemmas of Schooling*. Others have pointed to the same or similar features in policy making or decision making generally; see Lindblom, *Inquiry and Change*.

14. Changes in medical practice and the reduction of many common diseases in advanced industrial societies have greatly changed medical practice, so that many doctors and patients now deal with a broad range of social and psychiatric problems. Thanks to Alida Zweidler-McKay for helpful advice about these matters (personal communication).

15. William K. Muir, *Police: Streetcorner Politicians* (Berkeley: University of California Press, 1978).

16. Thanks again to Alida Zweidler-McKay for helpful advice (personal communication).

17. Oswald Spengler, among many others, argued that the pursuit of progress was essential to modern Western (he wrote "Faustian") civilization; Spengler, *The Decline of the West* (New York: Oxford University Press, 1991).

3. TEACHING

1. These issues are discussed throughout in Philip Cusick, *The Egalitarian Ideal and the American High School: Studies of Three Schools* (New York: Longmans, 1983), and in Theodore R. Sizer, *Horace's Compromise* (Boston: Houghton Mifflin, 1984).

2. Instruction refers to activities in which learning and teaching occur, whether attentive or not.

3. John Dewey, *How We Think* (New York: D. C. Heath, 1910), 35-36.

4. I owe the term "unnatural act," and much else in this discussion to Deborah Loewenberg Ball. See D. L. Ball and F. M. Forzani, "Teaching Skillful Teaching," *Educational Leadership*, 68, no. 4 (2010): 40-45, and Ball and Forzani, "The Work of Teaching and the Challenge for Teacher Education," *Journal of Teacher Education*, 60 (2009): 497-511.

5. D. L. Ball, "Building a System to Support Responsible Teaching Practice" (invited seminar, Institute for Education Sciences, U.S. Department of Education, Washington, DC, 2010).

6. Mark Twain, *Life on the Mississippi* (New York: Penguin, 1986), 72-109.

7. For a discussion of apprenticeships that are educational see John Seely Brown, Allan Collins, and Paul Duguid, "Situated Cognition and the Culture of Learning," in *Situated Learning Perspectives*, ed. Hillary McLellen, 19-44 (Englewood Cliffs, NJ: Educational Technology Publications, 1996).

8. Students' knowledge, as I use the term, includes the material in question and ideas and experiences that influence learners' ideas about the material. Culture and language thus bear on students' knowledge.

9. L. Shulman, "Knowledge and Teaching: Foundations of the New Reform," *Harvard Educational Review* 57 (1987): 1-22.

4. THE SOCIAL RESOURCES OF TEACHING

1. For discussion of this point see, David K. Cohen, Steven W. Raudenbush, and Deborah Lowenberg Ball, "Resources, Instruc-

tion, and Research," *Educational Evaluation and Policy Analysis* 25, no. 2 (Summer 2003): 119–142.

2. *Report of the National Reading Panel: Teaching Children to Read; An Evidence-Based Assessment of the Scientific Research Literature on Reading and Its Implications for Reading Instruction* (Washington, DC: U.S. Department of Health and Human Services, 2000).

3. National Governors Association and Council of Chief State School Officers, "Common Core State Standards Initiative Frequently Asked Questions," http://www.corestandards.org/ (downloaded February 3, 2010).

4. Nancy Koeber and Diane Stark Rentner, *States' Progress and Challenges in Implementing Common Core State Standards* (Washington, DC: Center on Education Policy, 2011), 1.

5. Thomas P. Rohlen, *Japan's High Schools* (Berkeley: University of California Press, 1983), 31–32.

6. R. E. Floden, A. C. Porter, W. H. Schmidt, and D. J. Freeman, "Don't They All Measure the Same Thing?: Consequences of Standardized Test Selection," in *Educational Testing and Evaluation: Design, Analysis, and Policy,* ed. E. L. Baker and E. S. Quellmalz (Beverly Hills: Sage, 1980); D. J. Freeman, T. M. Kuhs, A. C. Porter, R. E. Floden, W. H. Schmidt, and J. R. Schwille, "Do Textbooks and Tests Define a National Curriculum in Elementary School Mathematics?" *Elementary School Journal* 83 (1983): 501–513.

7. Theodore R. Sizer, *Horace's Compromise* (Boston: Houghton Mifflin,1984); Arthur Powell, Eleanor Farrar, and David K. Cohen, *The Shopping Mall High School* (Boston: Houghton Mifflin, 1985); P. Cusick, *The American High School and the Egalitarian Ideal* (New York: Longmans, 1984); W. Waller, *The Sociology of Teaching* (New York: J. Wiley, 1965).

8. Powell, Farrar, and Cohen, *Shopping Mall High School;* Cusick, *American High School and the Egalitarian Ideal.*

9. Interviews with Department of Education administrators in New South Wales, Australia, winter 1986.

10. Anthony Bryk, Valerie Lee, and Peter Holland, *Catholic Schools and the Common Good* (Cambridge, MA: Harvard University Press, 1993).

11. The AP program is operated by the College Board. The Board's most recent account reports that more than 1.5 million exams were taken by more than 938,000 students enrolled in thirty-four courses in more than 330,000 high schools ("The History of the AP Program," College Board, http://apcentral.collegeboard.com/apc/public/program/history/8019.html). Test Development Committees composed of high school and university teachers develop annual examinations in fifteen disciplines and prepare course descriptions and teacher manuals for these exams. The AP program aligns the student exams with curriculum taught to students, and even provides lists of suitable texts. But a relatively small proportion of U.S. high school students take any AP exam. Unlike national examinations in other countries, the AP exam is confined to university credit and placement, and not employment. Not all universities use AP, and the manner in which students' grades are used also varies among and within universities. These arrangements contrast with the uniform treatment of national examination scores by universities in other nations.

12. B. Rowan, "Commitment and Control: Alternative Strategies for the Organizational Design of Schools," in *Review of Research in Education,* ed. Courtney Cazden (Washington, DC: American Educational Research Association, 1990), vol. 16.

13. Stewart Purkey and Marshall Smith, "Effective Schools: A Review," *Elementary School Journal* 84, no 4. (1983): 427-452.

14. A. S. Bryk and M. E. Driscoll, *The High School as Community: Contextual Influences and Consequences for Students and Teachers* (Madison, WI: National Center on Effective Secondary Schools, University of Wisconsin, 1988). Bryk and Driscoll offer a larger vision that stresses shared values, concern for students' welfare, and faculty collegiality. In several articles Bryk and his associates probed the relations between various measures of schools as

"communities" and student performance. They defined community to include shared values, common curriculum and other
activities, and an ethos of "caring" for students. Schools that
placed high on these dimensions had lower dropout rates and
absenteeism, and slightly higher gains in mathematics achievement. See also A. Bryk, V. Lee, and J. B. Smith, "High School
Organization and Its Effects on Teachers and Students: An
Interpretation Summary of the Research," in *Choice and Control in
American Education,* ed. W. Clune and J. Witte, 178 (Newbury Park,
CA: Falmer, 1991) and Bryk, Lee, and Holland, *Catholic Schools and
the Common Good.*

15. Marshall Smith and Jennifer O'Day, "Systemic School Reform," in
    Politics of Education Association Yearbook 1990, ed. Susan Fuhrman
    and Betty Malen, 233–267 (London: Falmer Press, 1991).

16. David K. Cohen, Karen Gates, Joshua Glazer, Simona Goldin, and
    Donald Peurach, *Improvement By Design* (Chicago: University of
    Chicago Press, in press, 2012).

17. Jerome Bruner, *The Process of Education* (New York: Vintage, 1960),
    33. Horace Mann presented a version of these ideas in his *Annual
    Report for 1848* (Boston: Lee and Shephard, 1891), 303–319. John
    Dewey offered a similar view throughout *School and Society*
    (Chicago: University of Chicago Press, 1990).

18. In a search of the U.S. psychological literature in the last fifty years I
    found only a few titles that dealt with difficulty or risk in learning;
    they seem not to have been salient categories in learning research.

19. This assumes a ready supply of patients; lacking that supply,
    practitioners probably would be more cautious.

20. For discussion of these responses to reform, see David K. Cohen
    and Susan L Moffitt, *The Ordeal of Equality* (Cambridge, MA:
    Harvard University Press, 2009), 155–176.

21. David K. Cohen and Barbara Neufeld, "The Failure of High Schools
    and the Progress of Education," *Daedalus* 110, no. 3 (Summer 1981):
    69–90.

22. I distinguish interest from commitment, for to have an interest is not equivalent to having the will to pursue it.

23. The effects of selection also depend on the perspicacity of those who do the selecting and the strength of demand for the services. Selectivity becomes more difficult the closer the ratio of prospective clients to treatment vacancies approaches one or less than one.

24. Magnet schools have been tried on a limited basis, and researchers have not probed students' interests, so we have few serious estimates of students' academic interests. Hence there is no solid basis for estimating how many students from what sorts of backgrounds might be excluded from such acceptance schemes.

25. Selective acceptance can lead to contrary effects: some students may respond to membership in a selected group by thinking that there has been a mistake, that they do not belong, and that they cannot succeed.

26. This leverage often is qualified by other considerations. Some are economic. Having accepted student A, a school or university may be unable to replace his tuition with that of prospective student B because the time is late or the waiting list is empty, so it retains student A in the face of evidence that he is making no progress. Psychiatrists without waiting lists are in a similar position. Familiarity also may play a part; practitioners develop attachments to clients, which can inhibit decisions to stop treatment.

27. Gardiner Harris, "Talk Doesn't Pay, So Psychiatry Turns Instead to Drug Therapy," *New York Times,* March 5, 2011, 1, http://www.nytimes.com/2011/03/06/health/policy/06doctors.html?_r=1&nl=todaysheadlines&emc=tha3.

28. Cohen and Neufeld, "Failure of High Schools and the Progress of Education."

29. Enlistment often is less than fully voluntary. Students may enroll in a private school because parents push it and attendance is required, not because the students want it. Enlistment also can be ambivalent, even if it is entirely voluntary. But even ambivalent

voluntarism is more likely to produce committed clients than assigned enrollment in compelled improvement schemes, other things being equal.

30. Powell, Farrar, and Cohen, *Shopping Mall High School*, 222-232. Mutual choice does not work in a vacuum. Students in these schools also are more likely to work hard because they know that their work is likely to be rewarded with admission to desirable colleges and universities and desirable careers. Without such incentives, mutual choice would be less likely to create powerful resources of practice.

31. Bryk, Lee, and Holland, *Catholic Schools and the Common Good*.

32. Center for Research on Education Outcomes, *Multiple Choice: Charter School Performance in 16 States*, (Stanford, CA: Stanford University, 2009), 2-8, http://credo.stanford.edu/reports/MULTIPLE_CHOICE _CREDO.pdf.

33. Of course, teachers' willingness to take risks and face difficulty is sensitive to other circumstances that I discussed earlier with regard to consensus about results and communities of practice.

34. Ken Shimahara, "The Japanese Model of Professional Development: Teaching as Craft," *Teaching and Teacher Education* 14, no. 5 (1998): 451-462; Harold. W. Stevenson and James W. Stigler, *The Learning Gap: Why Our Schools Are Failing and What We Can Learn from Japanese and Chinese Education* (New York: Summitt Books, 1992).

35. Richard Hofstadter, *Anti-Intellectualism in American Life* (New York: Viking, 1962); Robert Lynd and Helen Lynd, *Middletown* (New York, Harcourt, Brace and Co., 1929), 181-222; Cusick, *American High School and the Egalitarian Ideal;* Powell, Farrar, and Cohen, *Shopping Mall High School*, 22-32, and 237-239.

36. Stevenson and Stigler, *Learning Gap*.

37. Hofstadter, *Anti-Intellectualism in American Life;* Lynd and Lynd, *Middletown;* Cusick, *American High School and the Egalitarian Ideal;* Powell, Farrar, and Cohen, *Shopping Mall High School*, 22-32, and 237-239.

38. Lynd and Lynd, *Middletown.*

39. Powell, Farrar, and Cohen, *Shopping Mall High School.* J. Bishop, "Incentives for Learning: Why American High School Students Compare So Poorly to Their Counterparts Overseas" (Cornell University, Center for Advanced Human Resource Studies Working Paper no. 89-09, 1989); J. Bishop, "Information Externalities and the Social Payoff to Academic Achievement" (Cornell University, Center for Advanced Human Resource Studies Working Paper no. 87-06, 1987).

40. Powell, Farrar, and Cohen, *Shopping Mall High School.*

41. J. Rosenbaum and T. Kariya, "Self-Selection in Japanese Junior High Schools: A Longitudinal Study of Student's Educational Plans," *Sociology of Education* 60 (July 1987): 168-180.

42. J. Bishop, "Incentives for Learning"; Rosenbaum and Kariya, "Self-Selection in Japanese Junior High Schools."

43. Paul T. Decker, Daniel P. Mayer, and Steven Glazerman, "The Effects of Teach For America on Students: Findings from a National Evaluation" (Princeton, NJ: Mathematica Policy Research Discussion Paper, 2004), 29-50, http://www.mathematica-mpr.com.

44. Brian Rowan, Richard Correnti, Robert J. Miller, and Eric M. Camburn, "School Improvement by Design: Lessons from a Study of Comprehensive School Reform Programs," in *Handbook of Education Policy Research,* ed. Gary Sykes, Barbara Schneider, and David Plank, with Timothy Ford, 637-651 (New York: Routledge, 2009).

5.   KNOWLEDGE AND TEACHING

1. Instruction is jointly produced by learners and teachers. That is how I understand the term, although I do not always repeat the entire sentence. It is jointly produced even when some students disrupt or refuse to participate. Instruction refers to jointly conducted practices of learning and teaching, even if they are conducted at a distance. Teachers usually have the lead role in

these joint productions, but that does not mean that they have the most important role; students do the learning, after all, and instruction affects students as well as teachers, each through the other.

2. John Dewey, *The Child and the Curriculum* (Chicago: University of Chicago Press, 1902).

3. Sir Michael Polanyi, *Personal Knowledge: Towards a Post-Critical Philosophy* (Chicago: University of Chicago Press, 1958).

4. Few American learning theorists seem to have noticed that learning often requires unlearning. This may have been due in part to the tabula rasa conception of mind that many philosophers and psychologists have embraced: if the mind is an empty vessel, then learning is a matter of filling it. Only if one sees the mind as constantly making sense of things, as Dewey did and recent cognitive psychologists do, might learning include how one sort of sense making interacts with and sometimes supplants another.

5. In U.S. elementary schools, teaching often offers no more than a compressed version of knowledge that is mechanically held, but even then it expresses a view of what it means to know something, and guides teachers' actions and interaction with students' work.

6. These differences in how knowledge is construed have been variously characterized. Commentators in education use terms like "rote," "procedural," and "mechanical" at one extreme and "understanding," "making sense," or "higher-order thinking" at the other. But the differences are difficult to define plainly because students "understand" mathematics even when they learn it as mechanical memorization, although they often understand it differently and less deeply than when they learn it as ideas about number and shape that they must explain and defend with mathematically legitimate terms of reference. The definitional difficulties increase when one grapples with cases in which teachers or students fashion some combination of the extreme

approaches. My aim is not to frame tight definitions. I seek to illustrate how modes of knowledge extension are affected by how knowledge is construed, so I am willing to accept fairly rough-and-ready characterizations of how knowledge for teaching varies.

7. The alternative approaches to knowledge extension depicted in Table 5.1 are often referred to under other headings, such as "presentation" and "explanation," but I avoid these because the nature of explanation varies across the approaches in the table. The categories I use are only a beginning in this area, but they are a bit more closely connected to knowledge extension than terms like "explanation."

8. Such work is especially easy because this version of knowledge is an old and familiar staple of both scholastic and popular culture in the United States. It is what most teachers were taught, and what many students learn outside school, so they need make no great intellectual changes to teach or learn.

9. That difference is not a matter of how much teachers know, but of how they know how to present knowledge. Some who construe history as an objective record of human events have a rich command of the material, while others have only a superficial grasp. Such differences in depth of knowledge influence the quality of what teachers extend to students, but they need not affect its synoptic character.

10. Learners often treat interpretive synopses as though they were procedures; they learn to reproduce the interpretations but do not question the ideas or apply them to related material.

11. The differences in teaching of this sort are not necessarily a consequence of how much teachers know. Many well-informed university instructors extend knowledge of calculus in a synoptic fashion, while others who are mathematically equally knowledge-able teach the same subject in more interpretive but synoptic ways. Nor does my account imply anything about how teachers

hold knowledge apart from instruction. Mathematicians who teach calculus as a synopsis of facts and procedures may work very differently in their research.

12. See examples and discussion of such work in the special issue of *Educational Evaluation and Policy Analysis* 12, no. 3 (Fall 1990). These mixed approaches to teaching figure in all the articles in this issue of the journal. See also L. Cuban, *How Teachers Taught* (New York: Longmans, 1984), 112–114 for his discussion of "hybrids."

6. INSTRUCTIONAL DISCOURSE

1. Any discourse opens some opportunities for acquaintance with students' knowledge and reduces others. I will discuss this topic in the next chapter.

2. John Dewey, *School and Society* (Chicago: University of Chicago Press, 1990).

3. See, for example, Horace Mann's "Report for 1848," in *Annual Reports of the Secretary of the Board of Education of Massachusetts*, 270–280 (Boston: Lee and Shepard, 1891).

4. Israel Scheffler, *Reason and Teaching* (Indianapolis: Bobbs-Merrill, 1973), 67–81.

5. Interviews with teachers and administrators concerning distance learning, Cowra Primary School and Western Regional Office, New South Wales, Australia, February–March 1988.

6. For example, recently developed computer-video systems open up opportunities for instructional discourse that would be difficult in the best lectures or discussions. See Magdalene Lampert and Deborah Lowenberg Ball, *Teaching, Multimedia and Mathematics: Investigations of Real Practice* (New York: Teachers College Press, 1998).

7. The complexity of such instruction would depend on its form. If teachers and students interact in a many-sided electronic mail network, the demands are greater than in two-way radio networks, but they are less than those in a computer-video network

in which teachers and students can see and hear each other in real time.

8. For some examples of this approach, see Arthur Powell, Eleanor Farrar, and David K. Cohen, *The Shopping Mall High School* (Boston: Houghton Mifflin, 1985); and Robert Everhart, *Reading, Writing, and Resistance: Adolescence and Labor in a Junior High School* (Boston: Routledge, Keegan Paul, 1983). These books depict seatwork as a desirable choice for many students who are little interested in instruction: the academic demands usually are modest, and they have plenty of opportunities for interaction among themselves as long as they are not overtly disruptive. But in some cases seatwork is one element in a complex and sophisticated instructional approach. When it is, considerable expertise is required. John Goodlad suggests, in *A Place Called School* (New York: McGraw Hill, 1984), that this approach to seatwork is uncommon, and that seatwork usually is part of a rather simplified form of instruction.

9. One reason that discipline and classroom management have become content-free topics in U.S. education is that the common forms of instructional discourse separate discipline from content by narrowing the discourse and student participation and thus expanding the borderland in which students can disrupt. The distinction between content and management reflects instructional practice at least as much as conventions of inquiry or professional discourse.

10. If students participate minimally or not at all in discussion, the instructional demands on them are thereby limited. Because some see discussion as an infringement on their privacy or on their wish to retain some distance from teachers and a class, they may resist or withdraw.

11. In French and British universities, students were not even expected to attend lectures. Professors could speak to nearly empty halls, and notes were passed around or sometimes published.

12. For examples, see Powell, Farrar, and Cohen, *Shopping Mall High School*, 184–207.

13. Notes on a grade 12 AP history class in North San Diego High School, spring 1984; notes on Grade 9 English top stream, Cowra High School, New South Wales, Australia, 1988.

14. It helps if teachers understand disputed points and puzzles in their disciplines because the better their students do, the more likely they are to happen on them. One distinguishing feature of this approach is that teachers and students embrace dispute about academic content, making it a central feature of discourse rather than closing it off.

15. For reports on the nature of such work, see M. Lampert, "Studying Teaching as a Thinking Practice," in *Thinking Practices,* ed. J. Greeno and S.G. Goldman (Hillsdale, NJ: Lawrence Erlbaum and Associates, 1998); Suzanne Wilson, Lee S. Shulman, and Anna Richert, "150 Different Ways of Knowing: Representations of Knowledge in Teaching," in *Exploring Teachers' Thinking,* ed. James Calderhead, 104–124 (London: Cassell, 1987); D. L. Ball, "With an Eye on the Mathematical Horizon: Dilemmas of Teaching Elementary School Mathematics," *Elementary School Journal* 93, no. 4 (1993): 373–397.

16. The term comes from Sir Michael Polanyi, "The Republic of Science," *Minerva* 1, (1962): 54–74, in which he discusses the nature of scientific discourse.

7. TEACHERS' ACQUAINTANCE WITH STUDENTS' KNOWLEDGE

1. I use the term "knowledge" as shorthand for the knowledge and beliefs that students bring to instruction and exhibit in their work and discourse.

2. Warren J. Colburn, "First Lesson in Arithmetic on the Plan of Pestalozzi with Some Improvements," in *Readings in the History of Mathematics Education,* ed. J. K. Bidwell and R. G. Clason (Washington, DC: National Council of Teachers of Mathematics, 1970).

3. A. Bronson Alcott, *Observations on the Principles and Methods of Infant Instruction* (Boston: Carter and Hendee, 1830); Elizabeth Palmer Peabody, *Record of a School* (Boston: J. Munro, 1835).

4. John Dewey, *School and Society* (Chicago: University of Chicago Press, 1990).

5. See, for example, Magdalene Lampert, *Teaching Problems and the Problems of Teaching* (New Haven, CT: Yale University Press, 2001), especially chapter 12.

6. The two approaches are not absolutely distinct or opposed. Teachers cannot look for signs of minds at work if they do not also check for congruence with their own ideas; such comparisons seem to be a critical element in thought of all sorts. But some teachers check only for congruence, while others use such checks as a subsidiary element in much more complex probing of students' knowledge.

7. T. Carpenter, E. Fennema, and M. Franke, "Cognitively Guided Instruction: A Knowledge Base for Reform in Primary Mathematics Instruction," *The Elementary School Journal* 97, no. 1 (1996): 3–20.

8. Jere Brophy, "Research on Teacher Effects: Uses and Abuses," *The Elementary School Journal* 89, no. 1 (1988): 3–22; Jere Brophy and Thomas Good, "Teacher Behavior and Student Achievement," in *Handbook of Research on Teaching,* 3rd ed., ed. M. C. Wittrock, 328–375 (New York: Macmillan Publishing, 1986).

9. M. Lampert, "Practices and Problems in Teaching Authentic Mathematics in School," in *Effective and Responsible Teaching: The New Synthesis,* ed. F. Oser, A. Dick, and J.-L. Patry, 295–314 (New York: Jossey-Bass, 1992); M. Lampert, "Teaching about Thinking and Thinking about Teaching," *Journal of Curriculum Studies* 16, no. 1 (1984): 1–18.

8. IMPROVE TEACHING

1. See, for example, David K. Cohen , "Revolution In One Class-room: The Case of Mrs. Oublier," *Educational Evaluation and Policy Analysis* 12, no. 3 (Autumn 1990): 311–329.

2. See, for example, Fred Hess, "Back to School," *American: The Journal of the American Enterprise Institute,* April 24, 2008, http://www.american.com/archive/2008/april-04-08/back -to-school.

3. These studies include Public Impact, *School Turnarounds: A Review of the Cross-Sector Evidence on Dramatic Organizational Improvement* (Chapel Hill, NC: Public Impact, Academic Development Institute, 2007); Ronald C. Brady, *Can Failing Schools Be Fixed?* (Washington, DC: Thomas B. Fordham Foundation, 2003); Emily Ayscue Hassell and Bryan C. Hassell, "The Big U-Turn," *Education Next,* Winter 2009, http://www.hoover.org/ publications/ednext/34686334.html; and Center on Education Policy, *Managing More Than a Thousand Remodeling Projects: School Restructuring in California* (Washington, DC: Center on Education Policy, 2008).

4. Center on Education Policy, *Managing More Than a Thousand Remodeling Projects,* 21.

5. See the studies cited in endnote 3, above.

6. See Michael J. Podgursky and Matthew G. Springer, "Teacher Performance Pay: A Review," http://web.missouri.edu/~podgurskym/papers_presentations/reports/Podgursky%20and%20Springer.pdf.

7. Heather C. Hill, "Evaluating Value-Added Models: A Validity Argument Approach," *Journal of Policy Analysis and Management* 28, no. 4 (2009): 700–709.

8. Ibid.

9. Two papers from the National Bureau of Economic Research discuss these issues: Jesse Rothstein, "Teacher Quality in Educational Production: Tracking, Decay, and Student Achievement" (National Bureau of Economic Research Working Paper no. 14442, March 2009); and Cory Koedel and Julian R. Betts,

"Value-Added to What? How a Ceiling in the Testing Instrument Influences Value-Added Estimation" (National Bureau of Economic Research Working Paper no. 14778, March 2009). See also Daniel McCaffrey, J. R. Lockwood, Tim R. Sass, and Kata Mihaly, "The Inter-temporal Variability of Teacher Effect Estimates," National Center on Performance Incentives, http://www.perfor manceincentives.org/ncpi-publications/Working-Papers/index .aspx.

10. Hill, "Evaluating Value-Added Models."

11. For a fuller discussion of accountability and its effects, see David K. Cohen and Susan L. Moffitt, *The Ordeal of Equality* (Cambridge, MA: Harvard University Press, 2010), chaps. 6 and 7.

12. Brian Rowan, Richard Correnti, Robert J. Miller, and Eric M. Camburn, "School Improvement by Design: Lessons from a Study of Comprehensive School Reform Programs," in *Handbook of Education Policy Research*, ed. Gary Sykes, Barbara Schneider, and David N. Plank, 637–651 (New York: Routledge, 2009).

13. National Governors Association, Council of Chief State School Officers, and Achieve, *Benchmarking for Success: Ensuring U.S. Standards Receive a World Class Education.* (Washington, DC: National Governors Association, Council of Chief State School Officers, and Achieve, 2008).

14. Maria Glod, "46 States, D.C. Plan to Draft Common Education Standards," *Washington Post,* June 1, 2009, http://www.kavanaugh software.com/index.php?option=com_content&view=article&id= 58:-46-states-dc-plan-to-draft-common-education-standards& catid=1:latest-news&Itemid=38.

15. Catherine Gewertz, "State School Boards Raise Questions about Standards," *Education Week,* February 3, 2010, http://www.edweek .org/ew/articles/2010/02/03/21nasbe.h29.html?tkn=SZBFY.

16. Ibid.

Index

Uncertainty and risk *(continued)*
knowledge, 174–175; congruence of
learning with teaching, 181, 183, 187;
inquiry-based learning, 184–185;
psychotherapy and, 208n9; educational research and, 213n18
Unions, 191–192
Universal acceptance, 79–80, 83–84
Universal programs, enlistment in,
89–90
Unlearning, 112–113, 217n4

Unnatural act, teaching as, 27, 114, 185
"Unpacked" instruction, 109–111, 112,
114, 120, 126–127, 128

Vicarious orientation to learners'
knowledge, 169, 172

Working conditions, 62
Written assignments, 36, 37

D0685874